A2 Music Listening Tests

Hugh Benham

and

Alistair Wightman

Rhinegold Education

239–241 Shaftesbury Avenue
London WC2H 8TF
Telephone: 020 7333 1720
Fax: 020 7333 1765

www.rhinegold.co.uk

Music Study Guides

GCSE, AS and A2 Music Study Guides (AQA, Edexcel and OCR)
GCSE, AS and A2 Music Listening Tests (AQA, Edexcel and OCR)
GCSE Music Study Guide (WJEC)
GCSE Music Listening Tests (WJEC)
AS/A2 Music Technology Study Guide (Edexcel)
AS/A2 Music Technology Listening Tests (Edexcel)
Revision Guides for GCSE (AQA, Edexcel and OCR), AS and A2 Music (AQA and Edexcel)

Also available from Rhinegold Education

Key Stage 3 Listening Tests: Book 1 and Book 2
AS and A2 Music Harmony Workbooks
GCSE and AS Music Composition Workbooks
GCSE and AS Music Literacy Workbooks
Romanticism in Focus, Baroque Music in Focus, Film Music in Focus,
Modernism in Focus, *The Immaculate Collection* in Focus, *Who's Next* in Focus,
Batman in Focus, *Goldfinger* in Focus, Musicals in Focus
Music Technology from Scratch

Rhinegold also publishes Choir & Organ, Classical Music, Classroom Music, Early Music Today, International Piano,
Music Teacher, Muso, Opera Now, Piano, The Singer, Teaching Drama, British and International Music Yearbook, British
Performing Arts Yearbook, British Music Education Yearbook, World Conservatoires, Rhinegold Dictionary of Music in Sound

Other Rhinegold Study Guides

Rhinegold publishes resources for candidates studying Drama and Theatre Studies.

First published 2010 in Great Britain by
Rhinegold Publishing Ltd
239-241 Shaftesbury Avenue
London WC2H 8TF
Telephone: 020 7333 1720
Fax: 020 7333 1765
www.rhinegold.co.uk

Rhinegold Publishing Ltd has used its best efforts in preparing this workbook. It does not assume, and hereby disclaims,
any liability to any party for loss or damage caused by errors or omissions in the Guide
whether such errors or omissions result from negligence, accident or other cause.

You should always check the current requirements of the examination, since these may change. Copies of the
Edexcel specification can be downloaded from the Edexcel website at www.edexcel.com.
Edexcel Publications telephone: 01623 467467, fax: 01623 450481, email: publications@linney.com.

Edexcel A2 Music Listening Tests
British Library Cataloguing in Publication Data.
A catalogue record for this book is available from the British Library.
ISBN: 978-1-906178-93-2
Printed in England by Halstan & Co Ltd, Amersham, Bucks.

Contents

The authors

Hugh Benham read Music and English at Southampton University, where he was awarded a PhD for his study of the music of John Taverner. He is a chair of examiners for GCE Music, an in-service trainer, church organist and writer, and formerly taught music in a sixth-form college. Hugh has contributed to *Music Teacher* and *Classroom Music* magazines, and is the author of *Baroque Music in Focus* (Rhinegold, 2007). His other writing includes two books on English church music, including *John Taverner: his Life and Music* (Ashgate, 2003), articles on early music, contributions to *The New Grove Dictionary of Music and Musicians* (2001) and *Die Musik in Geschichte und Gegenwart*, and a complete edition of Taverner for *Early English Church Music*.

Alistair Wightman read Music at Oxford and then York University, where he was awarded a D. Phil for his study of the music of Karol Szymanowski. He has worked in primary, secondary and further education, and is tutor in Aural Training at the Stafford Music Centre. He is also a freelance teacher and writer, and serves as a principal examiner in history and analysis in A-level music with one of the English awarding bodies. In addition to appearing as a pianist, both as a soloist and as a member of the Chiarina Trio, he continues to pursue his interests in Polish music, his publications including several books and articles devoted to Tadeusz Baird, Karlowicz and Szymanowski.

Acknowledgements

The authors would like to thank the consultant Paul Terry and the Rhinegold editorial and design team of Harriet Power, Silvia Schreiber and Richard Gumbley for their expert support in the preparation of this book.

Audio tracks

Please note that there is no CD to accompany this book. All of the tracks used for these tests are available to download from iTunes as one 'album' or iMix.

To purchase and download the iMix, please go to the *Edexcel A2 Music Listening Tests (second edition)* page at www.listeningtests.co.uk, where you will find a direct link to the iTunes store.

On the same webpage you will find a PDF titled 'Rhinegold Education Listening Tests Instructions', which provides help on using iTunes to play the tracks for these tests, as well as advice on alternative sources to iTunes for finding or downloading the tracks.

Introduction

What this book is for

This book is to help you to do as well as you possibly can in the Further Musical Understanding exam for Edexcel A2 Music (Unit 6). Here you will find various listening tests for Section A of the Unit 6 exam, with answers, and also advice and specimen questions to help you prepare for Sections B and C.

How to use this book

> **If you are taking the exam in 2010**, first use the listening tests labelled '2010' in Section A (pages 9–13 and 25–31). The listening tests labelled '2011' will however provide you with additional valuable practice. In Sections B and C, read the general advice and then concentrate on the questions labelled '2010' (pages 39–40).
> **If you are taking the exam in 2011**, first use the listening tests labelled '2011' in Section A (pages 14–18 and 32–38). The listening tests labelled '2010' will however provide you with additional valuable practice. In Sections B and C, read the general advice and then concentrate on the questions labelled '2011' (pages 39–40).

For the listening tests in Section A, this book contains spaces in which to write your answers, and for the Aural Awareness questions we have provided the necessary skeleton scores. The music that you must listen to in order to answer the Section A questions can be accessed from iTunes. Use the section of each track that is indicated by the timing at the top of each question.

You may instead use CD recordings, but the timings of these might not be right, and some of the features on which the questions are based may be less clear than in the recommended iTunes performances.

> For help on using iTunes for these listening tests, see page 4 or go to the *Edexcel A2 Music Listening Tests (second edition)* page at www.listeningtests.co.uk.

When working through the exercises, you might want to keep to exam conditions as closely as possible, for example by listening to the music for each test the regulation number of times, observing the appropriate lengths of pauses and so on (there's more on this below on pages 7–8). But, early on in the course especially, you can use the tests as practice and learning material rather than as pretend exam questions – for example, by listening to excerpts more times than possible in the exam. Try working through some tests a second time once you have had a chance to forget the answers.

Examination requirements

You must read the full examination requirements as set out in the specification (or syllabus) for Edexcel A2 Music. Your teacher will have a copy, but the information can also be accessed from the Edexcel website (www.edexcel.com). **Remember that specifications can change *and* that some requirements are specific to particular years.** It is your teacher's responsibility and yours to know all about the relevant examination requirements.

Examiners' top tips

Apart from as much listening experience as you have time for, and plenty of practice at each type of test, examiners recommend the following:

1. **Learn the correct technical words.** You must know these because they sometimes appear in the questions and should be used in your answers.

> Some sources of information on technical words are given on the next page, in the introduction to Section A.

2. **Read each question thoroughly** and do exactly what it requires. Correct and relevant information gets marks; irrelevant information does not (even if it is true).

3. **Believe your ears!** In listening tests, write about what you actually hear, rather than what you expect to hear.

4. **Note how many marks are available for each question.** For example, if there is a bracketed three (3) after part of a question, this means that three marks are available, and that you will generally need to make three points in your answer.

5. **Avoid getting bogged down,** especially on questions that carry only a single mark. Near the end of your exam, you may have time to return (refreshed) to answers originally left incomplete.

6. **Manage your time carefully.** You have two hours for the Unit 6 exam. Section A is structured for you – you listen to a CD with all the music you need and there are pauses between the excerpts for you to write your answers. For Sections B and C together you will probably have just under an hour and a half. As Section B carries 26 marks, and Section C 36 marks, it is sensible to spend longer on the latter than on the former. There's no hard-and-fast rule, but you might spend 35–40 minutes on the two 13-mark questions that make up Section B, and the remainder of your time (probably some 50–55 minutes) on the extended essay in Section C.

Section A: Aural Analysis

There are two questions – entitled 'Comparison' and 'Aural Awareness' – which are worth 10 and 18 marks respectively (together they make up 28 of the 90 marks for the whole Unit 6 paper).

Comparison question

For comparison questions, you have to identify and comment on musical features from two excerpts, comparing and contrasting them as required. In the exam you will hear each excerpt three times, in the order A, B; A, B; A, B. There will not be a break between A and B, but there will be a pause after each hearing of Excerpt B. The first two pauses will be 30 seconds in length, and the third (during which you complete your answers) will last for 2 minutes.

It may not always be feasible to follow this pattern exactly when you're working with iTunes or separate CDs. In particular it may be difficult to manage a quick changeover from Excerpt A to Excerpt B – unless you ask someone to help you with such practicalities.

In comparison questions, be ready to think about the following musical features:

➢ Melody
➢ Rhythm and metre
➢ Harmony
➢ Tonality
➢ Texture
➢ Form (structure)
➢ Instrumental and/or vocal forces.

> Remember especially that 'tonality' usually means 'key' in Unit 6 – not tone quality or anything like that. 'Harmony' refers to individual chords and successions of chords, and is not an alternative term for accompaniment. For further brief comments on these features, see the glossary (page 72) and recent examiners' reports for Edexcel A2 Music. See also the *Dictionary of Music in Sound* (Rhinegold, 2001).

In each comparison question, you will be asked to place the excerpts in their historical, social or cultural context (notably by identifying genres, composers and dates of composition). The excerpts will be taken from a piece (or from two different pieces) that may be unfamiliar to you. The music chosen will, however, be related in some way to one or more of the set works that you study for Section B and/or Section C.

Although this leaves a vast number of possibilities, it does help to suggest a structure for the listening part of the course. If there is a set work by Bach or Stravinsky, for example, you might listen to other music by the composer in question. If you are studying a trio sonata or fugue, it is a good idea to hear other trio sonatas (and similar chamber-music genres) or other fugues.

The more music you hear, the better equipped you will be to name genres, composers and dates. In fact, the only way to do this is to compare what you are trying to identify with what you have previously heard. Listening to music that you don't know and may not like isn't easy – little and (very) often is a good maxim. There's always the chance, if you listen widely and are open-minded, that from time to time you will come across something unexpectedly wonderful!

Aural awareness question

What we have just said applies equally to the aural awareness question, because again you will be asked to comment on the music's context.

In addition, you will be asked in each test to recognise chords and keys, and complete a simple aural dictation task (that is, to write down in musical notation something you have just heard played or sung). You will have to listen to only one excerpt of music, which in the exam you will hear five times, with the following pauses: 30 seconds after the first hearing, 1 minute after the second, 1 minute after the third, 30 seconds after the fourth, and 3 minutes after the fifth. To help you with the aural awareness question, there is a single- or two-stave skeleton score of the music.

Aural dictation may come easily to you or you may need a lot of practice, depending partly on how familiar you are with staff notation. It is a skill worth persevering with, apart from anything to do with the exam: for example, it can be very useful to write down musical ideas when there is a risk of forgetting them and when no means of making a recording is available.

Start by working through the dictation examples on pages 19–24: these are not available on iTunes, so ask someone to play them to you (or download them from www.listeningtests.co.uk). It is easier to begin with these separate, short examples than with the tests that are embedded in longer pieces of music. Your teacher can easily make up dictation tests for you when you have run out of them in this book. Try writing your own for your friends to do.

To be able to recognise chords and keys is useful in many forms of music-making, including composing and improvising. You may need a lot of practice with it: one good plan is to work or rework the activities in chapter 2 of the *AS Music Harmony Workbook* (Rhinegold, 2008).

Question 1: Comparison (2010)

Test 1   **A: 0:00–0:57, B: 0:00–0:52**

The following questions require you to compare and contrast two excerpts of music (which we will call A and B) from the same work. Listen to both excerpts three times in the order A, B; A, B; A, B.

As explained on page 7, Excerpt B should follow Excerpt A without a break each time. There should be a 30-second pause after the first and second hearings of Excerpt B. Allow yourself 2 minutes after the third hearing of Excerpt B in order to complete your answers.

(a) Contrast the use of string instruments in the two excerpts.

A - legato. Solo violin. Intro included many instruments. When solo violin comes only one other instrument is heard as an accompaniment. B-Strings are faster. A lot of them are playing staccato notes, with some legato →solo. solo →. (other way around) **(3)**

> The question tells you that both excerpts have strings – so you need to comment on some different ways in which the strings are deployed, in particular referring to any solo instruments.

(b) Name the type of longer work from which these excerpts come.

Concerto **(1)**

> Your response to (a) above may help you answer (b).

(c) How do the two excerpts differ in texture?

B has a contrapuntal texture. – immitative.
A has melody dominated homophony **(2)**

(d) Indicate whether the statements below are true or false by placing a cross in the appropriate box.

(i)   Only Excerpt A is in compound time.   TRUE ☒   FALSE ☒

(ii) Descending chromatic melodic lines
appear in both excerpts.   TRUE ☒   FALSE ☒   **(2)**

(e) Put a cross in the box next to the name of the composer of these excerpts.

☒ **A** Corelli   ☒ **B** Gabrieli   ☒ **C** Monteverdi   ☒ **D** Vivaldi   **(1)**

(f) Suggest a possible year of composition.

1650 x 1750 **(1)**

(Total 10 marks)

Test 2   **A: 0:00–1:01, B: 0:00–1:03**

The following questions require you to compare and contrast two excerpts of music from the same work. Listen to each excerpt three times in the order A, B; A, B; A, B; with pauses as indicated on page 9.

(a)   Put a cross in the box next to the **one** statement below which is true.

☒   **A** Both excerpts begin in a major key

☒   **B** Both excerpts begin in a minor key

☒   **C** Excerpt A begins in a major key; Excerpt B begins in a minor key

☒   **D** Excerpt A begins in a minor key; Excerpt B begins in a major key   **(1)**

(b)   Identify **two** differences between the vocal melodic lines of the two excerpts.

   1.   ....

   2.   ....   **(2)**

(c)   Comment on the tempi of the two excerpts.

   ....

   ....   **(2)**

> 'Tempi' is plural of 'tempo' (musical speed or pace).

(d)   Name **two** types of chord used only in Excerpt B, which make its harmony more tense than the harmony of Excerpt A.

   1.   ....

   2.   ....   **(2)**

(e)   Name the type of longer work from which Excerpts A and B are taken.

   ....   **(1)**

(f)   Put a cross in the box next to the year in which these excerpts were composed.

   ☒   **A** 1735   ☒   **B** 1770   ☒   **C** 1805   ☒   **D** 1840   **(1)**

> You will get a mark for a correct answer to (f) even if, later on, you contradict it when answering question (g). Try though, as far as possible, to think about questions on years and composers together, so that the answer to one helps you with the answer to the other.

(g)   Put a cross in the box next to the name of the composer of these excerpts.

   ☒   **A** Beethoven   ☒   **B** Handel   ☒   **C** Mozart   ☒   **D** Wagner   **(1)**

(Total 10 marks)

Test 3   **A: 0:00–0:54, B: 0:00–1:18**

The following questions require you to compare and contrast two excerpts of music from the same work. You will hear each excerpt three times in the order A, B; A, B; A, B; with pauses as indicated on page 9.

(a)   Much of Excerpt A is based on a motif with three different pitches, the first two of which are B and C. What is the third pitch?

....   **(1)**

(b)   Describe **one** way in which the composer treats this motif.

....   **(1)**

(c)   Comment on the melodic writing in the first (slow) section of Excerpt B.

....

....   **(2)**

> The question asks for comment on 'melodic writing' (e.g. on stepwise or leaping movement, or how motifs are used), not for identification of instruments. You will have the chance to comment on instrumentation in part (e).

(d)   What wind instrument, accompanied by strings, plays a solo in the second part of Excerpt A (after the staccato rising scales)?

....   **(1)**

(e)   Describe the instrumentation and texture of the first (slow) section of Excerpt B.

....

....

....   **(3)**

(f)   Suggest a possible composer of these excerpts.

....   **(1)**

(g)   Put a cross in the box next to the year in which these excerpts were composed.

☒ **A** 1910   ☒ **B** 1940   ☒ **C** 1970   ☒ **D** 2000   **(1)**

(Total 10 marks)

Test 4   **A: 0:00–1:26, B: 0:00–1:25**

The following questions require you to compare and contrast two excerpts of music from the same work. You will hear each excerpt three times in the order A, B; A, B; A, B; with pauses as indicated on page 9.

(a) Compare and contrast the metre and rhythm of the two excerpts.

....

....

....

.... **(4)**

> When you listen without a score, it can be impossible to identify the time signature exactly (in particular, to tell the difference between $\frac{2}{2}$ and $\frac{4}{4}$, or $\frac{2}{4}$ and $\frac{3}{2}$). If you write $\frac{2}{4}$ and the score says $\frac{4}{4}$, you won't be marked wrong, but more general observations are preferable, such as 'duple or quadruple metre'.

(b) Excerpt A begins by repeating a short section. Its opening idea continues to dominate much of the rest of the excerpt. Comment on the use of repetition in Excerpt B.

....

.... **(2)**

(c) How does the tonality of Excerpt B differ from the tonality of Excerpt A:

(i) At the start of each extract? ....

(ii) At the end of each extract? .... **(2)**

> Questions on tonality do not expect you to identify aurally the actual keys used (e.g. F major or B minor). They just expect references to use of major or minor, and/or to change(s) of key.

(d) Put a cross in the box next to the year in which these excerpts were composed.

☒ **A** 1776   ☒ **B** 1826   ☒ **C** 1876   ☒ **D** 1926   **(1)**

(e) Put a cross in the box next to the name of the composer of these excerpts.

☒ **A** Beethoven   ☒ **B** Debussy   ☒ **C** Mendelssohn   ☒ **D** Mozart   **(1)**

(Total 10 marks)

Test 5   **A: 0:00–1:07, B: 0:00–1:03**

The following questions require you to compare and contrast two excerpts of music in the same musical style. You will hear each excerpt three times in the order A, B; A, B; A, B; with pauses as indicated on page 9.

(a)   Name **two** rhythmic features common to both excerpts and typical of the style.

1.   ....

2.   ....   **(2)**

(b)   In which excerpt do several melodic phrases end with a descending, stepwise motif of three notes?

....   **(1)**

(c)   Comment on the instrumentation and textures in the introductions to these excerpts.

....

....

....

....   **(4)**

(d)   Name the solo instrument heard at the end of Excerpt B.

....   **(1)**

(e)   Put a cross in the box next to the style that best describes these excerpts.

☒ **A** Bebop   ☒ **B** Traditional jazz   ☒ **C** Ragtime   ☒ **D** Twelve-bar blues   **(1)**

(f)   Put a cross in the box next to the year in which these excerpts were recorded.

☒ **A** 1912   ☒ **B** 1927   ☒ **C** 1942   ☒ **D** 1957   **(1)**

(Total 10 marks)

Question 1: Comparison (2011)

Test 1   **A: 0:00–1:11, B: 0:00–1:06**

The following questions require you to compare and contrast two excerpts of music (which we will call A and B) from the same work. Listen to both excerpts three times in the order A, B; A, B; A, B.

As explained on page 7, Excerpt B should follow Excerpt A without a break each time. There should be a 30-second pause after the first and second hearings of Excerpt B. Allow yourself 2 minutes after the third hearing of Excerpt B in order to complete your answers.

(a) What vocal resources are used in Excerpt A?

....

.... **(2)**

(b) Compare and contrast the vocal resources used in Excerpt B with those used in Excerpt A.

....

.... **(2)**

> The expression 'vocal resources' in parts (a) and (b) refers to the types of voices (not instruments) used, and to the use of soloists and/or choir.

(c) Name the wind instrument that has a solo part in Excerpt A.

....   **(1)**

> Solo instrumental parts in Baroque music are often called 'obbligato' (note spelling with double 'b'), to stress that they are vital to the musical texture, and therefore obligatory.

(d) How do the excerpts differ in texture?

....

.... **(2)**

(e) Name the type of longer work from which these excerpts are taken.

....   **(1)**

(f) Suggest a possible composer for these excerpts.

....   **(1)**

(g) Put a cross in the box next to the year in which these excerpts were composed.

☓ **A** 1686   ☓ **B** 1726   ☓ **C** 1766   ☓ **D** 1806   **(1)**

(Total 10 marks)

Test 2   **A: 0:00–1:14, B: 0:00–1:16**

The following questions require you to compare and contrast two excerpts of music from different works by the same composer. You will hear each excerpt three times in the order A, B; A, B; A, B; with pauses as indicated on page 14.

(a) Name **two** different instruments heard in Excerpt A but not in Excerpt B.

    1. ....

    2. .... **(2)**

(b) Contrast the textures of the two excerpts.

    ....

    .... **(2)**

(c) How does the harpsichord part in Excerpt B differ in function from that of Excerpt A?

    ....

    .... **(2)**

(d) How does the melodic writing at the **beginning** of the two excerpts differ?

    ....

    .... **(2)**

> You won't hear the beginning of each excerpt in immediate succession. So it may help, when you listen to Excerpt A, to jot down one or two things about the beginning, to refresh your memory when you get to Excerpt B.

(e) Suggest a year of composition for these two works.

    .... **(1)**

(f) Put a cross in the box next to the name of the composer of these excerpts.

    ☒ **A** J. S. Bach   ☒ **B** Corelli   ☒ **C** Handel   ☒ **D** Vivaldi   **(1)**

(Total 10 marks)

Test 3   **A: 0:00–1:11, B: 0:00–1:07**

The following questions require you to compare and contrast two excerpts of music from different works by the same composer. You will hear each excerpt three times in the order A, B; A, B; A, B; with pauses as indicated on page 14.

Both excerpts are in fast triple metre.

(a)   Describe the texture and instrumentation of the opening four-bar phrase of Excerpt A.

    Texture ....

    Instrumentation .... **(2)**

(b)   In terms of texture and instrumentation, how is the opening four-bar phrase of Excerpt B:

    (i)   **Similar** in texture to the opening phrase of Excerpt A?

      ....

    (ii)   **Different** in instrumentation from the opening phrase of Excerpt A?

      .... **(2)**

(c)   What type of woodwind instrument is heard **only** in Excerpt B?

    .... **(1)**

(d)   Indicate **two** ways in which the tonality of Excerpt B differs from that of Excerpt A.

    1.   ....

    2.   .... **(2)**

> Questions on tonality do not expect you to identify aurally the actual keys used (e.g. F major or B minor). They just expect references to use of major or minor, and/or to change(s) of key.

(e)   Excerpt A is from a Minuet. From what type of movement, also in triple time, is Excerpt B?

    .... **(1)**

(f)   Name the type of multi-movement work from which both excerpts come.

    .... **(1)**

(g)   Put a cross in the box next to the name of the composer of these excerpts.

    ☒ **A** Brahms   ☒ **B** Haydn   ☒ **C** Schubert   ☒ **D** Tchaikovsky   **(1)**

(Total 10 marks)

Test 4   A: 0:00–1:33, B: 0:00–1:12

The following questions require you to compare and contrast two excerpts of music from the same work. You will hear each excerpt three times in the order A, B; A, B; A, B; with pauses as indicated on page 14.

(a) Contrast the melodic writing in the opening vocal phrases of each excerpt.

....

.... **(2)**

> Concentrating on a single phrase from each excerpt may seem difficult, but each phrase is heard more than once (to different words), which should help.

(b) Contrast the handling of rhythm and metre in each excerpt.

....

....

.... **(3)**

> When you listen without a score, it can be impossible to identify the time signature exactly (in particular, to tell the difference between $\frac{2}{2}$ and $\frac{4}{4}$, or $\frac{2}{4}$ and $\frac{2}{2}$). If you write $\frac{2}{2}$ and the score says $\frac{4}{4}$, you won't be marked wrong, but more general observations are preferable, such as 'duple or quadruple metre'.

(c) Comment on the tonality of each excerpt.

Excerpt A ....

Excerpt B .... **(2)**

(d) Name the type of longer work from which these excerpts are taken.

.... **(1)**

(e) Put a cross in the box next to the year in which these excerpts were composed.

☒ **A** 1917   ☒ **B** 1937   ☒ **C** 1957   ☒ **D** 1977   **(1)**

(f) Put a cross in the box next to the name of the composer of these excerpts.

☒ **A** Bernstein   ☒ **B** Gershwin   ☒ **C** Cole Porter   ☒ **D** Lloyd Webber **(1)**

(Total 10 marks)

Test 5   **A: 0:00–1:21, B: 0:00–1:22**

The following questions require you to compare and contrast two excerpts of music from different works by the same composer. You will hear each excerpt three times in the order A, B; A, B; A, B; with pauses as indicated on page 14.

(a) Put a cross in the box next to the term describing the type of scale widely used in the melodic material of both excerpts.

☒ **A** Minor   ☒ **B** Modal   ☒ **C** Pentatonic   ☒ **D** Whole-tone   **(1)**

(b) Compare and contrast the harmony of the two excerpts.

....

....

....   **(3)**

(c) Describe the textures of Excerpt A.

....

....

....   **(2)**

(d) Using a single word, describe the texture at the beginning of Excerpt B.

....   **(1)**

(e) What type of non-European music influenced the composer in these excerpts?

....   **(1)**

(f) Put a cross in the box next to the decade in which these excerpts were composed.

☒ **A** 1870s   ☒ **B** 1900s   ☒ **C** 1930s   ☒ **D** 1960s   **(1)**

(g) Suggest a possible composer for these excerpts.

....   **(1)**

(Total 10 marks)

Dictation Exercises

The exercises that follow are to help in the early stages of practice by isolating the dictation task from other aspects of Question 2 (Aural Awareness). Nevertheless, to begin getting used to hearing dictation in context, each exercise has a little given material before and after the part(s) you have to complete.

> In a few cases, tests have been very slightly adapted from the original pieces of music, which are identified in the answers section on page 49.

To ease you into the process of dictation, in tests 1–5 we have asked you to supply note values in some places and pitches elsewhere, not both at the same time. Where pitches have to be supplied, the note values are shown; where note values are to be added, the pitches are given.

> Before tackling tests 1–5 you should have worked with more straightforward and shorter examples.
> Even supplying just one or two missing note values or one or two pitches can be valuable in the very early stages. Try 'self-dictation': hear a melody in your head, or sing it aloud, and try writing it down.

In each of tests 6–21, as in the exam, a passage is left entirely blank, for you to supply both note values and pitches. You are free to experiment and discover what method of working suits you best, but it may help to start with note values and then add pitches (or to work the other way round), rather than try to supply both melody and rhythm at once. The first time you hear a test, it can help just to decide how many notes there are – perhaps by putting a dot over the stave for each note you hear. You might then want to go straight to using conventional notation, but if it helps, start by indicating pitch with letter names (e.g. A, B, C♯, D), or rhythm by using a grid to show where each note comes in relation to the beat or pulse.

> Almost all tests use the treble clef, like Edexcel's sample question, and as appears likely in future assessments. The bass-clef tests are a reminder that these are not actually excluded by the specification. For additional bass-clef practice, ask someone to play other tests one or two octaves lower, taking care to avoid too many leger lines.

Practicalities

Your teacher, or someone else, can play a test from the answers section on page 49, while you have in front of you the actual test with blank bar(s) from pages 20–24. Tests can be played on the piano or any other suitable instrument. A tempo mark is suggested, but in early practice the music can be played more slowly if necessary. The person playing the test can begin by sounding the tonic chord of the key in which the test starts, but bear in mind that this will not happen in the exam – you must identify the key from the context.

If there is no one at hand to play the tests for you, go to the Rhinegold website (www.rhinegold.co.uk) and download the MP3 files to your computer or iPod.

Alternatively, you may be able to access the music for some tests on CDs or from iTunes. This would enable you to hear the underlying harmony, as happens in the exam, but there can be difficulties with this method, such as locating the precise bars you have to work with.

It does not matter in the early stages how many times you hear a test, but as you approach the exam, limit the number of playings to five.

To monitor your progress, each time you do a test, count up the number of pitches and/or the number of note values you get correct, and turn these into a percentage. Regard 40% or more of the total as good progress, and 70% or more as very encouraging.

Where a solution indicates that there are, for example, nine notes to be supplied, you need to reckon on *nine note values and nine pitches*. A 'note' is a single sound: occasionally a 'note' may have to be written as two symbols tied together.

Examiners' top dictation tips

➤ Identify the key at the beginning of each piece of dictation. Does it change as the test goes on?

➤ Some tests require you to add pitches that carry accidentals. Such accidentals are vital – if you miss them out, the notes that should have had them are counted as wrong.

➤ Sometimes a pattern that you need to add can be worked out from one of the given passages. Be alert to the possibility of straight repetition or melodic sequence.

Test 1

Supply the missing note values in bars 2–3 and 8–9.

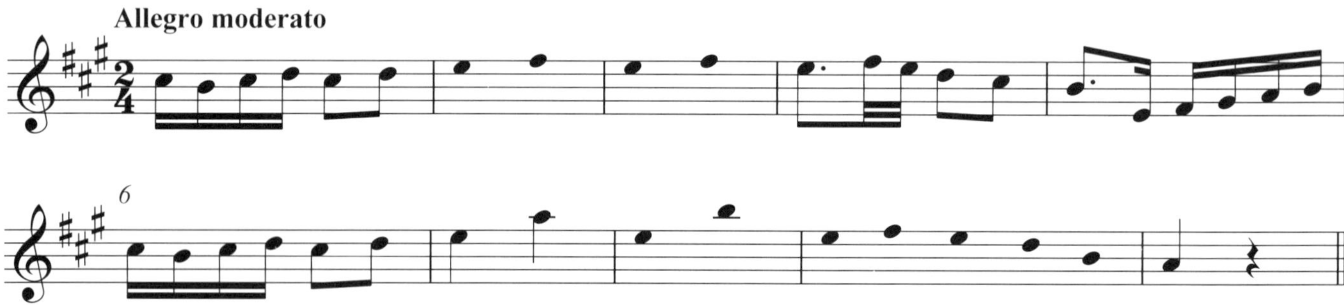

Test 2

Supply the missing pitches in bars 3 and 7–8.

Test 3

Supply the missing note values in bars 3–4, and the missing pitches in bars 7–8.

Test 4

Supply the missing note values in bars 3–4, and the missing pitches in bars 7–8.

Test 5

Supply the missing note values in bars 3–4, and the missing pitches in bars 6–7.

Test 6

Supply the missing notes in bars 4–5.

Test 7

Supply the missing notes from bar 5 (third crotchet beat) to bar 7.

Note that this test does not end in the key in which it begins. You need to include a crucial accidental.

Test 8

Supply the missing notes from bar 3 to bar 4 (second crotchet beat).

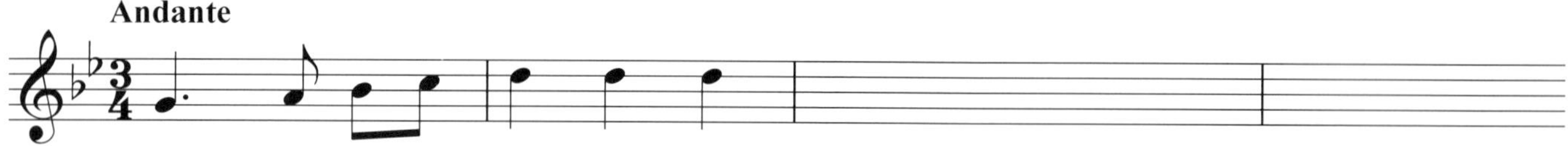

Test 9

Supply the missing notes in bars 2–4.

Test 10

Supply the missing notes from bar 4 (last crotchet beat) to bar 6 (second crotchet beat).

Test 11

Supply the missing notes in bars 2–3.

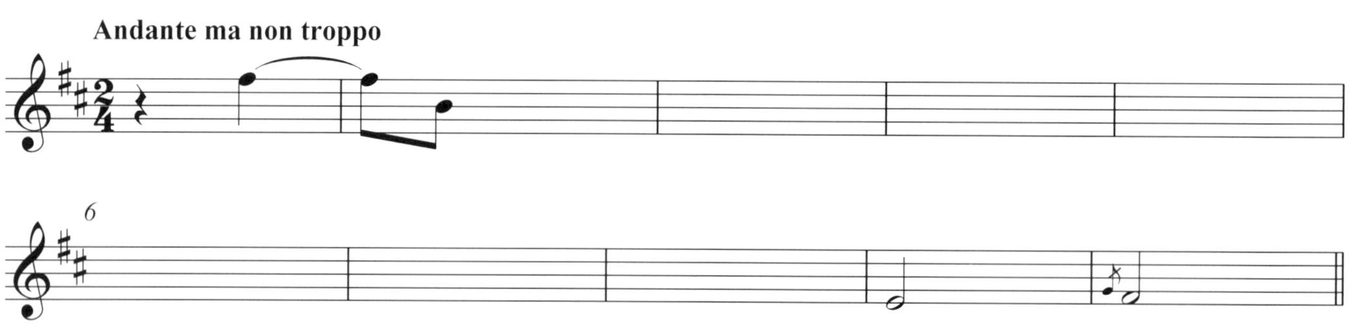

Test 12

Supply the missing notes from bar 2 (second crotchet beat) to bar 8.

The gap between the given opening and ending may look rather wide, but you have to supply only nine notes.

Test 13

Supply the missing notes in bars 2–3.

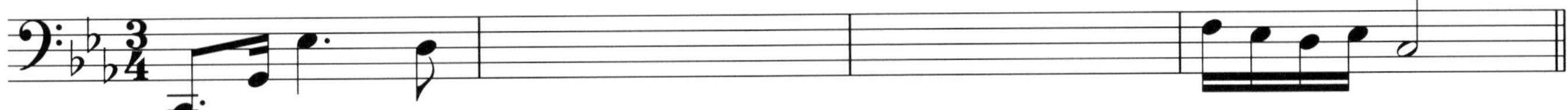

Test 14

Supply the missing notes from bar 1 (fourth crotchet beat) to bar 3 (second crotchet beat).

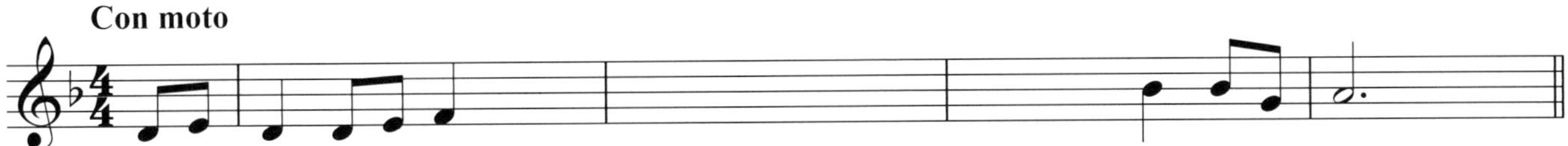

Test 15

Supply the missing notes in bars 2–4.

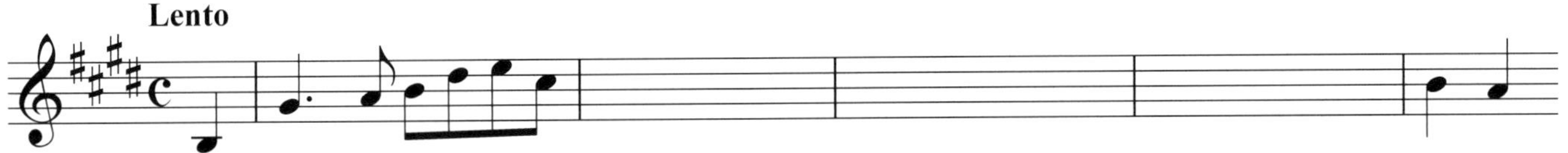

Test 16

Supply the missing notes from bar 2 to bar 4 (first crotchet beat).

Test 17

Supply the missing notes in bars 5–7.

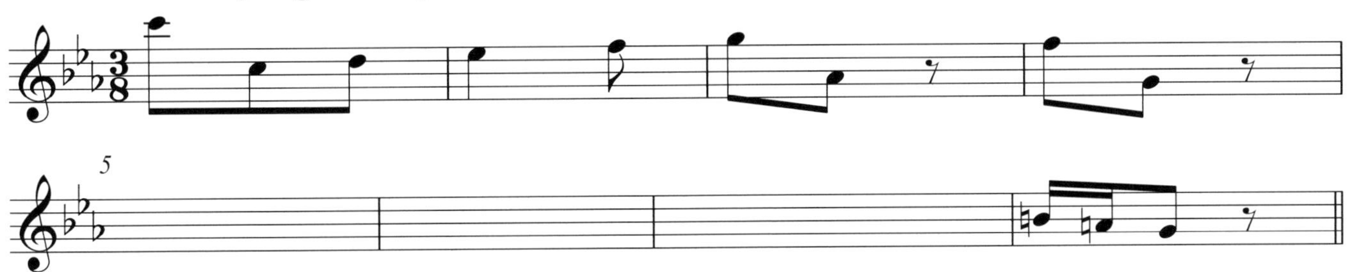

There are three quaver rests in bars 5–7.

Test 18

Supply the missing notes from bar 2 (fourth quaver beat) to bar 4.

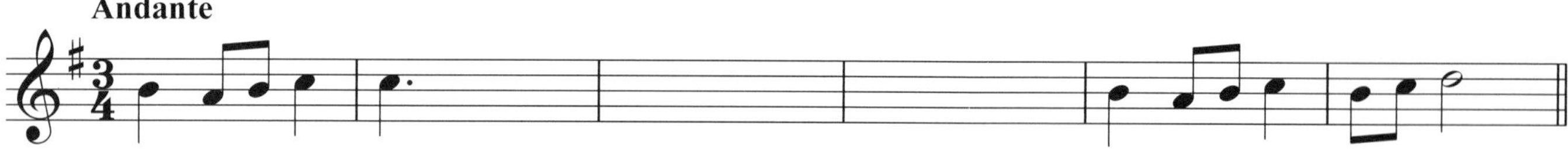

Test 19

Supply the missing notes in bar 3.

Test 20

Supply the missing notes from bar 3 (third crotchet beat) to bar 4.

Test 21

Supply the missing notes from bar 5 (last crotchet beat) to bar 7.

Here's something a little lighter and easier to finish with!

Question 2: Aural Awareness (2010)

Test 1   0:00–2:39

You will hear an excerpt of music five times. The playings will be separated by pauses:

➢ After the first playing, there should be a 30-second pause
➢ After the second playing, there should be a 1-minute pause
➢ After the third playing, there should be a 1-minute pause
➢ After the fourth playing, there should be a 30-second pause
➢ After the fifth and final playing, allow yourself 3 minutes to complete your answers.

There is a skeleton score on page 1 of the score insert, which you must follow as you listen to the music for this test.

(a)   Write out the missing melody line in bars 35–37. You may work in rough on the skeleton score, but you must copy your answer onto the stave below.

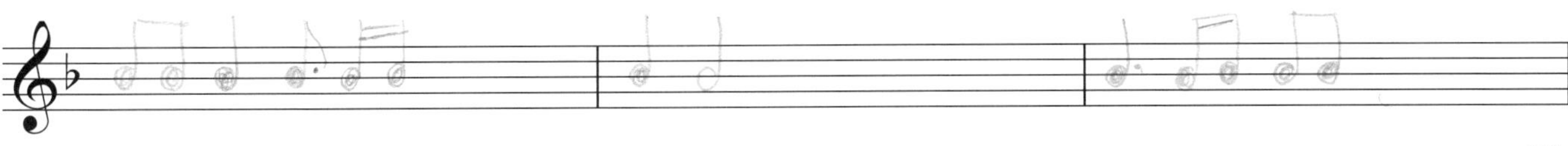

                                                                                (8)

> This dictation exercise comes at the end of the excerpt, so that it is relatively easy to remember the music you have to write down during the pauses that follow the various playings. It doesn't move very fast either, which should give you time to think about *accidentals* (for example, the one at the end of bar 35).

(b)   (i)   Identify the **three** chords indicated in bars 7–8.

            Chord A .....G. minor.....II......✓......

            Chord B .....F. Major......I......✓......

            Chord C .....D. major.....V......✓......   **(3)**

      (ii) Identify the key and cadence in bar 10 and in bars 23–24.

            Bar 10:   Key   ......F. major....✓.................

                         Cadence   ......Perfect....✓.................

            Bars 23–24: Key   ......C. Major....✓.................

                         Cadence   ......Imperfect....✓................   **(4)**

> When asked to name a key, you are free to give its precise name (e.g. E♭ major) or its relationship to the tonic key (e.g. subdominant).

                                                                          Turn over

(c) (i)   Put a cross in the box next to the type of piece from which this excerpt is taken.

     ☒ **A** Anthem   ☒ **B** Chorale   ☒ **C** Mass   ☒ **D** Recitative   **(1)**

(ii) Name the composer of this excerpt.

Bach > (-Huydn/Mozart)

    (1)

> Questions on composers and dates are marked separately – you can get one wrong and still get a mark for the other if it's right. But try wherever possible to use your answer to the composer question to cross-check your answer to the date question and vice versa.

(iii) Put a cross in the box next to the year in which this music was composed.

     ☒ **A** 1749   ☒ **B** 1779   ☒ **C** 1809   ☒ **D** 1839   **(1)**

(Total 18 marks)

Test 2   **0:00–2:31**

You will hear an excerpt of music five times. The playings will be separated by pauses as indicated on page 25.

There is a skeleton score on pages 2–3 of the score insert, which you must follow as you listen to the music for this test.

(a)   Write out the missing melody line in bars 30–32. You may work in rough on the skeleton score, but you must copy your answer onto the stave below.

(8)

(b)   (i)   Identify the **two** chords in bar 8, first and second crotchet beats.

Chord A ....

Chord B ....   (2)

(ii)   Identify the key and cadence in bars 11–12 and 21–23.

Bars 11–12 ....

Bars 21–23 ....   (4)

(iii)   Identify the type of chord used in bar 18, second crotchet beat.

....   (1)

> The expression 'type of chord' means that you don't have to give a roman numeral, as in (b) (i). For a 'type of chord' question, the answer instead might be something along the lines of 'augmented sixth', 'diminished seventh' or 'Neapolitan sixth'.

(c)   (i)   From what type of multi-movement work is this excerpt taken?

....   (1)

(ii)   Put a cross in the box next to the name of the composer of this music.

☒ **A** Bach   ☒ **B** Beethoven   ☒ **C** Brahms   ☒ **D** Haydn   (1)

(iii)   Suggest a possible year of composition for this work.

....   (1)

(Total 18 marks)

Test 3   **0:00–2:17**

You will hear an excerpt of music five times. The playings will be separated by pauses as indicated on page 25.

There is a skeleton score on page 4 of the score insert, which you must follow as you listen to the music for this test.

(a)   Complete the melody line in bars 26–28. You may work in rough on the skeleton score, but you must copy your answer onto the stave below.

(8)

(b)   (i)   Name the type of dissonance used in the following places:

Bar 6, first dotted-crotchet beat   ....

Bar 14, first quaver beat   ....   (2)

> The expression 'type of dissonance' covers passing notes, auxiliary notes, suspensions, appoggiaturas, etc.

(ii)   Identify the **three** chords indicated in bars 9 to 11.

Chord A (bars 9–10) ....

Chord B (bar 11, first dotted-crotchet beat)   ....

Chord C (bar 11, second dotted-crotchet beat) ....   (3)

(iii)   Name the key to which the music modulates in bars 25–26.

....   (1)

(iv)   Identify the cadence in bars 31–32.

....   (1)

(c)   (i)   Name the type of work from which this excerpt is taken.

....   (1)

(ii)   Put a cross in the box next to the name of the composer of this music.

☒ **A** Bach   ☒ **B** Beethoven   ☒ **C** Mendelssohn   ☒ **D** Mozart   (1)

(iii)   Put a cross in the box next to the year when this music was composed.

☒ **A** 1756   ☒ **B** 1786   ☒ **C** 1816   ☒ **D** 1846   (1)

(Total 18 marks)

Test 4   **0:00–2:19**

You will hear an excerpt of music five times. The playings will be separated by pauses as indicated on page 25.

There is a skeleton score on pages 6–7 of the score insert, which you must follow as you listen to the music for this test.

(a)   Write out the melody line of bars 14–16. You may work in rough on the skeleton score, but you must copy your answer onto the stave below.

(8)

(b)   (i)   Identify the type of chord used in bars 25 and 26.

Chord A (whole of bar 25) ....

Chord B (whole of bar 26) ....   (2)

(ii)   Identify the key of the music at bar 27.

....   (1)

(iii)   Identify the cadence and key in bars 43–44, and in bars 54–55.

Bars 43–44 ....

Bars 54–55 ....   (4)

(c)   (i)   From what type of extended work is this excerpt taken?

....   (1)

(ii)   Put a cross in the box next to the name of the composer of this music.

☒ **A** Bach   ☒ **B** Haydn   ☒ **C** Mozart   ☒ **D** Weber   (1)

(iii)   Put a cross in the box next to the year when this music was first performed.

☒ **A** 1731   ☒ **B** 1761   ☒ **C** 1791   ☒ **D** 1821   (1)

(Total 18 marks)

Test 5   **0:00–2:42**

You will hear an excerpt of music five times. The playings will be separated by pauses as indicated on page 25.

There is a skeleton score on pages 8–9 of the score insert, which you must follow as you listen to the music for this test.

(a) Write out the melody line of bars 14–15. You may work in rough on the skeleton score, but you must copy your answer onto the stave below.

                                                                                                        (8)

(b) (i) Identify the chords used in bars 10 and 11.

        Chord A (whole of bar 10) ....

        Chord B (whole of bar 11) ....   (2)

   (ii) Identify the key in bars 18 (second beat) to 21 (first beat).

        ....   (1)

   (iii) Identify the chord or type of chord indicated in each of the following cases.

        Chord C (bars 22–23)   ....

        Chord D (last two quavers of bar 24) ....

        Chord E (beginning of bar 25)   ....   (3)

   (iv) What type of dissonance is used in bar 29 (quavers 4 and 5)?

        ....   (1)

   (v) Name the harmonic device used in the bass part from bar 34 to the beginning of bar 40.

        ....   (1)

(c) (i) Put a cross in the box next to the name of the composer of this music.

        ☒ **A** Beethoven   ☒ **B** Brahms   ☒ **C** Mendelssohn   ☒ **D** Mozart   (1)

   (ii) Suggest a year of composition for this piece.

        ....   (1)

                                                                                    (Total 18 marks)

Test 6   **0:00–2:27**

You will hear an excerpt of music five times. The playings will be separated by pauses as indicated on page 25.

There is a skeleton score on pages 10–11 of the score insert, which you must follow as you listen to the music for this test.

(a)   Write out the melody line of bar 21 (third crotchet beat) to bar 23 (first crotchet beat). You may work in rough on the skeleton score, but you must copy your answer onto the stave below.

> Think carefully about the first note. (Clue: it has an accidental, and is a note heard a little earlier in the piece.) The start of a dictation question is vital, because if you get the first note wrong it may be difficult to capture some of what follows. Sometimes, however, you can work backwards from the first note in the skeleton score that follows the gap you have to fill.

(8)

(b)   (i)   Identify the key at the marked passages in:

      Bars 8–9   ....

      Bars 12–13 ....   (2)

      (ii)   Identify the type of chord used in each of the following locations:

      Bar 8, second minim beat   ....

      Bar 11, third crotchet beat ....   (2)

      (iii) Explain the relationship between the marked passage in bars 17–19 and the preceding passage (bracketed in bars 14–16).

      .... (1)

      (iv) Identify the cadence in bar 24.

      ....   (1)

      (v)   Identify the **two** chords in bar 26.

      Chord A ....

      Chord B ....   (2)

(c)   (i)   From what type of work is the excerpt taken?

      ....   (1)

      (ii)   Put a cross in the box next to the name of the composer of this music.

      ☒ **A** Corelli   ☒ **B** Handel   ☒ **C** Purcell   ☒ **D** Vivaldi   (1)

(Total 18 marks)

Question 2: Aural Awareness (2011)

Test 1   **0:00–1:44**

You will hear an excerpt of music five times. The playings will be separated by pauses:

- ➢ After the first playing, there should be a 30-second pause
- ➢ After the second playing, there should be a 1-minute pause
- ➢ After the third playing, there should be a 1-minute pause
- ➢ After the fourth playing, there should be a 30-second pause
- ➢ After the fifth and final playing, allow yourself 3 minutes to complete your answers.

There is a skeleton score on pages 12–13 of the score insert, which you must follow as you listen to the music for this test.

(a) Complete the melody line of bars 44–48. You may work in rough on the skeleton score, but you must copy your answer onto the stave below.

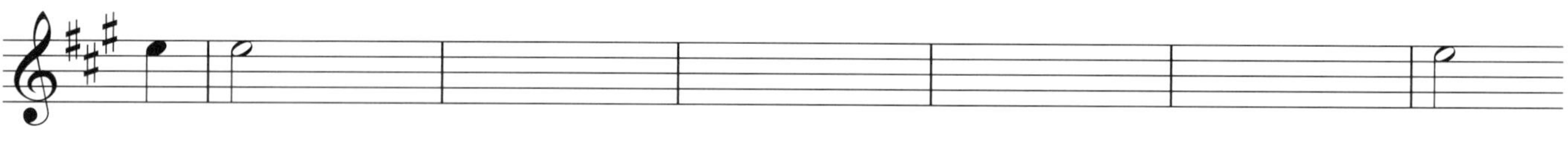

                                                                                          (8)

(b) (i) Give the roman numeral of the chord heard from bar 6 (last crotchet beat) to bar 8 (third crotchet beat).

         ....   **(1)**

> This chord lasts long enough for you to have a really good chance to listen to it! The given pitches, D♯ and B, provide you with valuable clues. And there's a second chance to hear the chord later in the excerpt when some of the opening music is repeated.

   (ii) Name the key and the cadence in the two following locations:

      1. Bar 11 to bar 12 (second crotchet beat)

          Key   ....

          Cadence ....

      2. Bar 15 to bar 16 (third crotchet beat)

          Key   ....

          Cadence ....   **(4)**

   (iii) Name the type of chord used at the start of bar 29.

         ....   **(1)**

> The expression 'type of chord' means that you don't have to give a roman numeral, as in (b) (i). For a 'type of chord' question, the answer instead might be something along the lines of 'augmented sixth', 'diminished seventh' or 'Neapolitan sixth'.

(iv) Bars 30–34 have two short phrases whose harmony is similar. Give one way in which the harmony of the second phrase differs from the harmony of the first.

.... **(1)**

(c) (i) Put a cross in the box next to the type of longer work from which this excerpt is taken.

☒ **A** Magnificat   ☒ **B** Mass   ☒ **C** Oratorio   ☒ **D** Passion   **(1)**

(ii) Put a cross in the box next to the name of the composer of this music.

☒ **A** Handel   ☒ **B** Haydn   ☒ **C** Mendelssohn ☒ **D** Purcell   **(1)**

(iii) Put a cross in the box next to the year in which this composition was first performed.

☒ **A** 1717   ☒ **B** 1757   ☒ **C** 1798   ☒ **D** 1837   **(1)**

(Total 18 marks)

Test 2 0:00–2:23

You will hear an excerpt of music five times. The playings will be separated by pauses as indicated on page 32.

There is a skeleton score on pages 14–15 of the score insert, which you must follow as you listen to the music for this test.

(a) Write out the melody line of bars 24–25. You may work in rough on the skeleton score, but you must copy your answer onto the stave below.

(8)

(b) (i) Name the type of dissonance that is heard three times in the lower part in bars 9–11.

.... **(1)**

'Types' of dissonance include anticipations, appoggiaturas, auxiliary notes, passing notes and suspensions. For information on types of dissonance, see the glossary, page 72.

(ii) Identify the **two** chords in bar 36.

Chord A ....

Chord B .... **(2)**

(iii) Name the key in bars 41–44, and the type of cadence.

Key ....

Cadence .... **(2)**

(iv) Identify the key through which the music passes:

In bars 46 to 48 (first crotchet beat) ....

In bar 62 .... **(2)**

(v) Identify the key at the end of the excerpt.

.... **(1)**

(c) (i) Of what type of piece is this music the beginning?

.... **(1)**

(ii) Put a cross in the box next to the name of the composer of this music and the approximate date of composition.

   ☒ **A** J. S. Bach, 1730   ☒ **B** Mozart, 1790

   ☒ **C** Mendelssohn, 1830   ☒ **D** Brahms, 1890   **(1)**

(Total 18 marks)

Test 3   **0:00–2:47**

You will hear an excerpt of music five times. The playings will be separated by pauses as indicated on page 32.

There is a skeleton score on pages 16–17 of the score insert, which you must follow as you listen to the music for this test.

> Brahms' song was originally in the key of E major. The skeleton score here is in D major, which matches the recommended recording.

(a) Complete the melody line of bars 49–53. You may work in rough on the skeleton score, but you must copy your answer onto the stave below.

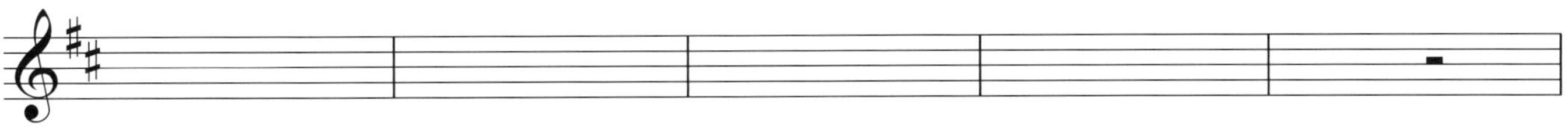

(8)

> Although the melody line you have to add extends for more than four bars, there are no more than twelve notes to write. Clue: melodic sequence is used. Write down the first note of bars 49, 50 and 51 to give a kind of framework, before adding in the remainder of bars 49 and 50.

(b) (i)   Identify the chord heard in bar 3. .... **(1)**

    (ii) Identify each of the following cadences:

        Cadence A (bars 6–7)   ....

        Cadence B (bars 54–55)   ....

        Cadence C (bars 55–57) .... **(3)**

    (iii) Identify the key in:

        Bars 10–14 ....

        Bars 25–27 .... **(2)**

    (iv) Precisely identify the harmonic device employed in bars 13–20.

        .... **(1)**

    (v) Identify the chord heard in bar 34, first minim beat. It is in the tonic minor key, D minor.

        .... **(1)**

(c) (i)   Put a cross in the box next to the type of song heard in this test.

      ☒ **A** Aria   ☒ **B** Ballad   ☒ **C** Lied   ☒ **D** Mélodie   **(1)**

    (ii) Suggest a possible composer for this song. .... **(1)**

(Total 18 marks)

Test 4   **0:00–2:02**

You will hear an excerpt of music five times. The playings will be separated by pauses as indicated on page 32.

There is a skeleton score on pages 18–20 of the score insert, which you must follow as you listen to the music for this test.

(a) Complete the melody line of bar 36. You may work in rough on the skeleton score, but you must copy your answer onto the stave below.

                                                                                  (8)

(b) (i) Complete the sentence below:

         In bar 8 there is a(n) .... cadence in

         the key of ....   **(2)**

     (ii) Name the key in:

         Bars 12–14 ....

         Bar 22   ....   **(2)**

     (iii) What type of chord is heard in bar 18, last crotchet beat?

         ....   **(1)**

     (iv) What type of cadence is heard in bars 24–26?

         ....   **(1)**

     (v) Precisely identify the harmonic device used in bars 29–31.

         ....   **(1)**

(c) (i) This excerpt is from the first movement of a work in three movements. What kind of work is this?

         ....   **(1)**

     (ii) Put a cross in the box next to the name of the composer of this music.

         ☒ **A** J. S. Bach   ☒ **B** Brahms   ☒ **C** Chopin   ☒ **D** Haydn   **(1)**

     (iii) Suggest a year of composition.

         ....   **(1)**

                                                                          (Total 18 marks)

Test 5   **0:00–2:19**

You will hear an excerpt of music five times. The playings will be separated by pauses as indicated on page 32.

There is a skeleton score on page 21 of the score insert, which you must follow as you listen to the music for this test.

(a)   Write out the missing melody line in bar 14. You may work in rough on the skeleton score, but you must copy your answer onto the stave below.

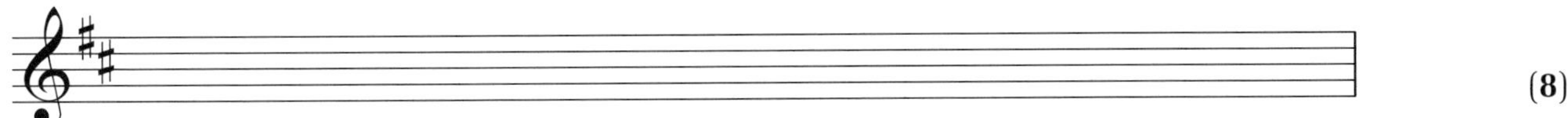

              (8)

(b) (i)   Identify the key and cadence in bars 4 and 18.

            Bar 4: Key   ....

                     Cadence ....

             Bar 18: Key   ....

                     Cadence ....   **(4)**

    (ii)   Identify the chord or type of chord used at each place indicated in bar 7.

            Chord A ....

             Chord B ....

             Chord C ....   **(3)**

(c) (i)   Put a cross in the box next to the type of longer work from which this excerpt is taken.

          ☒ **A** Anthem   ☒ **B** Mass   ☒ **C** Opera   ☒ **D** Passion   **(1)**

    (ii)   Put a cross in the box next to the name of the composer of this music.

          ☒ **A** Bach   ☒ **B** Handel   ☒ **C** Haydn   ☒ **D** Purcell   **(1)**

    (iii) Put a cross in the box next to the year when this music was first performed.

          ☒ **A** 1667   ☒ **B** 1697   ☒ **C** 1727   ☒ **D** 1757   **(1)**

(Total 18 marks)

Test 6 0:00–2:15

You will hear an excerpt of music five times. The playings will be separated by pauses as indicated on page 32.

There is a skeleton score on pages 22–23 of the score insert, which you must follow as you listen to the music for this test.

(a) Write out the melody line of bars 6–9. You may work in rough on the skeleton score, but you must copy your answer onto the stave below.

(8)

For additional practice, after you have completed questions (a)–(c), try adding the missing melody line of bars 36–38.

(b) (i) Identify the chords indicated in bars 13–16.

Chord A ....

Chord B .... (2)

(ii) Identify the key of bars 22–26, and the cadence.

Key ....

Cadence .... (2)

(iii) Name the type of chord heard at the end of bar 39.

.... (1)

(iv) Identify the key through which the music passes in bars 47–49.

.... (1)

(v) Identify precisely the harmonic device used in bars 53–60.

.... (1)

(c) (i) What contrapuntal device is used in the opening bars of this excerpt?

.... (1)

(ii) Suggest a year of composition for this music.

.... (1)

(iii) Put a cross in the box next to the name of the composer of this music.

☒ **A** Bach   ☒ **B** Beethoven   ☒ **C** Berlioz   ☒ **D** Brahms (1)

(Total 18 marks)

Section B: Music in Context

Section B is about the set works for Area of Study 3: Applied Music. You will find the works for the year of your examination listed in the requirements for Unit 6 in the specification.

Section B will contain three questions, of which you have to answer any two. They will be labelled 3(a), 3(b) and 3(c), and each will refer to a different set work. In each case you will be asked to identify particular musical features and indicate how these help to place the piece in its social and historical context.

Answers may be written in note form (bullet points, etc.), in continuous prose, or indeed in some mixture of the two. You may find that use of continuous prose helps you to express your meaning most clearly and fully, and it is a useful preparation for Section C, where this form of writing must be used. Whatever your style of writing, make sure that everything is legible, correct in terms of spelling, punctuation and grammar, intelligible and well organised: you will be assessed on the 'quality of written communication'.

Remember to:

1.   Answer the question

   ➢   Include everything that you consider is relevant, even if it seems obvious
   ➢   Avoid everything that is irrelevant, even if it is correct.

2.   Give an example wherever possible, whenever you make a point

   ➢   An example nearly always requires a bar reference (for example, if your point is 'The composer uses diminished seventh chords,' add 'as in bar 34, beat 2').

The specimen questions below give you some idea of the way these questions are framed. For sample answers, see page 66.

> Additional information on answering this type of question (and Section C questions) is available in the *Edexcel A2 Music Revision Guide* (Rhinegold, 2010).

2010

What features of instrumentation, harmony and tonality would enable you to establish a date of composition for Gabrieli's *Sonata pian' e forte* (*NAM* 14)? **(13)**

2011

ET: Flying Theme (*NAM* 45) accompanies a depiction of an aerial bike-ride. What features of the score make it particularly suitable for this purpose? **(13)**

Section C: Continuity and Change in Instrumental Music

Section C is about the set works from Area of Study 1: Instrumental Music. Note that these are different from the ones you studied for Unit 3 (at AS level). You will find the works for the year of your examination listed in the requirements for Unit 6 in the specification.

Section C will contain two questions, of which you have to answer only one. They will be labelled 4(a) and 4(b). Each option in the specimen Question 4 that was published when the specification was launched deals with three works, and we have assumed in this book that this will be the pattern in the actual exam. Each option in Question 4 will focus on one or more named musical features, asking you to demonstrate how these help us to see continuity and change from one work to another. Discussion will be limited to the named works – it is not necessary to refer to works from outside the anthology.

Answers must be essays written in continuous prose, and quality of written communication will be assessed. As in Section B, make sure that everything is legible, correct in terms of spelling, punctuation and grammar, intelligible and well organised. As your answer will be in essay form, you may wish to include an introductory paragraph and a concluding one, rather than just starting straight in with relevant information as you might in Section B. But to be worthwhile, an introduction or a conclusion must do more than just repeat what is written in the body of the essay.

Remember to:

1. Answer the question

    ➢ Include everything that you consider is relevant, even if it seems obvious
    ➢ Avoid everything that is irrelevant, even if it is correct.

2. Give an example wherever possible, whenever you make a point

    ➢ An example nearly always requires a bar reference (for example, if your point is 'The composer uses diminished seventh chords,' add 'as in bar 34, beat 2').

The specimen questions below give you some idea of the way these questions are framed. For sample answers, see page 67.

2010

Beethoven: Septet in E♭, Op. 20, movement I (*NAM* 17)
Louis Armstrong and his Hot Five: *West End Blues* (*NAM* 48)
Tippett: Concerto for Double String Orchestra, movement I (*NAM* 6)

Compare and contrast melody and harmony in the three pieces listed above.   (**36**)

2011

Haydn: Symphony No. 26 in D minor, movement I (*NAM* 2)
Brahms: Piano Quintet in F minor, Op. 34, movement III (*NAM* 18)
Duke Ellington and his Orchestra: *Black and Tan Fantasy* (*NAM* 49)

Compare and contrast instrumentation and textures in the above works.   (**36**)

Question 2: Aural Awareness (2010)

Test 1 (2010)

Test 2 (2010)

Adagio
p
f
p
p
p
(b) (i) chords
A   B
(b) (ii) key and cadence
(b) (iii)
type of chord
(b) (ii) key and cadence
sf
sf
sf
sf
Presto
p

26
30
(a) notate melody
33
f
sf
sf
39
sf
sf
44

Test 3 (2010)

Adagio
(b) (i) dissonance
(b) (ii) chord A
chord B
chord C
p
(b) (i) dissonance
f
(b) (iii) key
(a) notate melody
(b) (iv) cadence

Blank page

Test 4 (2010)

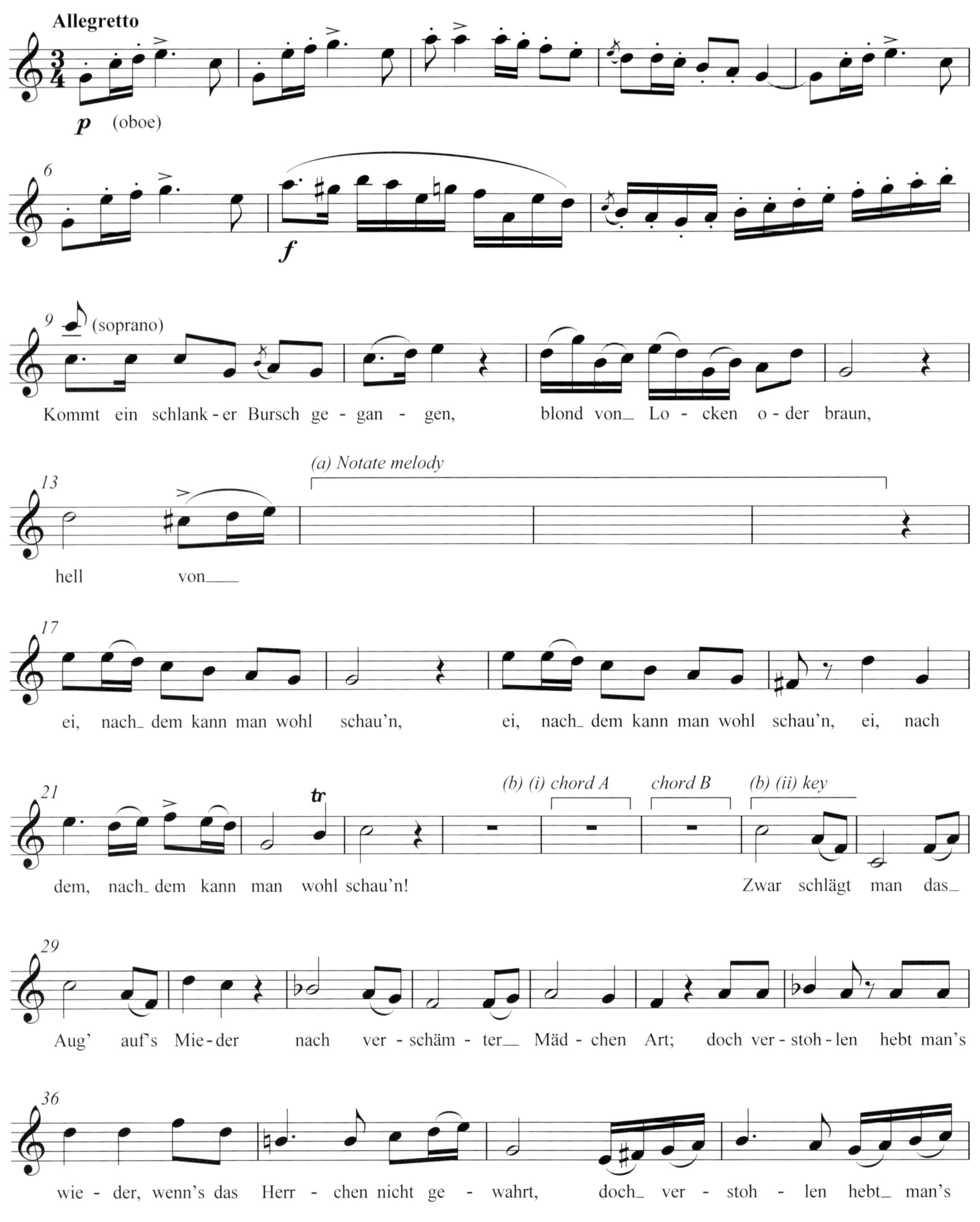

Allegretto
p   (oboe)
f
(soprano)
Kommt ein schlank - er Bursch ge - gan - gen, blond von Lo - cken o - der braun,
(a) Notate melody
hell von
ei, nach dem kann man wohl schau'n, ei, nach dem kann man wohl schau'n, ei, nach
(b) (i) chord A   chord B   (b) (ii) key
tr
dem, nach dem kann man wohl schau'n! Zwar schlägt man das
Aug' auf's Mie - der nach ver - schäm - ter Mäd - chen Art; doch ver - stoh - len hebt man's
wie - der, wenn's das Herr - chen nicht ge - wahrt, doch ver - stoh - len hebt man's

(b) (iii)
cadence and key
wie - der, wenn's das Herr - chen nicht ge - wahrt, es nicht ge - wahrt, es nicht ge -
wahrt. Soll - ten ja sich Bli - cke fin - den,
nun, was hat das auch für Noth? man wird drum nicht gleich er - blin - den,
(b) (iii) cadence and key
wird man auch ein we - nig roth, ein we - nig roth, ein we - nig
roth. Blick - chen hin und Blick her - ü - ber,
bis der Mund sich auch was traut. Er seufzt:
Schön - ste! Sie spricht: Lie - ber! Bald heisst's Bräu - ti - gam und Braut,
bald heisst's Bräu - ti - gam und Braut, Bräu - ti - gam und Braut.

Test 5 (2010)

Andante sostenuto
sf
p
p
cantabile
(b) (i) chord A
chord B
(a) notate melody
(b) (ii) key
(b) (iii) chord C

chord D
chord E
(b) (iv)
dissonance
sf
dim.
p
mf
(b) (v) harmonic device in bass
pp

Test 6 (2010)

Adagio
Do - mi - ne__ De - us,
A - gnus De - i, Fi - li - us Pa - tris.   Do - mi - ne
De - us,   Do - mi - ne   De - us,   A - gnus De - i, Fi - li - us Pa -
tris.   Qui tol - lis pec - ca - ta, Do - mi - ne__ De - us, Rex Cae - le - stis,   qui
(b) (i) key
(b) (ii) type of chord
(b) (ii) type of chord
(b) (i) key
(b) (iii)
tr

(b) (iii) relationship with preceding bracketed passage
16
tol - lis pec - ca - ta, Do - mi - ne__ Fi - li U - ni - ge -ni - te, qui tol - lis pec -
19
(a) notate melody
ca - ta, Do - mi - ne__ De - us, Do - mi - ne__ De - us,
22
(b) (iv) cadence
qui tol - lis pec - ca - ta mun - di,
25
(b) (v) chord A   chord B
mi - se - re - re, A - gnus De - i, mi - se - re - re,
28
tr
Fi - li - us Pa - tris, mi - se - re - re__ no - bis,

Question 2: Aural Awareness (2011)

Test 1 (2011)

25
ho - ly beams___   The gloom - y   shades   of   an - cient

(b) (iii)
29 type of chord
(b) (iv) one harmonic difference
night.   The   first   of days   ap - pears,   the   first   of days   ap-

34
pears.   Now cha - os   ends,   and

38
or - der, and   or - der   fair   pre - vails,   Now cha - os ends,
tr

(a) Notate melody
43
now   cha - os   ends,   and   or -

46
vails.

Test 2 (2011)

(b) (iii) key and cadence
(b) (iv) key
(b) (iv) key
(b) (v) key
tr

Test 3 (2011)

Ziemlich langsam [quite slow]
(piano)
(voice)
(b) (i) chord
p
Geuss nicht so laut der lieb-ent-flamm-ten Lie-der ton-
(b) (ii) cadence A
(b) (iii) key
rei-chen Schall vom Blü-ten-ast des A-pfel-baums her-nie-der, o
Nach-ti-gall! Du tö-nest mir mit dei-ner sü-ssen Keh-le die
(b) (iv) harmonic device
Lie-be wach; denn schon durch bebt die Tie-fen mei-ner See-le dein
(b) (iii) key
schmel-zend 'Ach'; dein schmel - zend 'Ach',
Dann flicht der Schlaf von neu-em die-ses La-ger, ich
(b) (v) chord in D minor
star-re dann mit nas-sem Blick und to-ten bleich und ha-ger

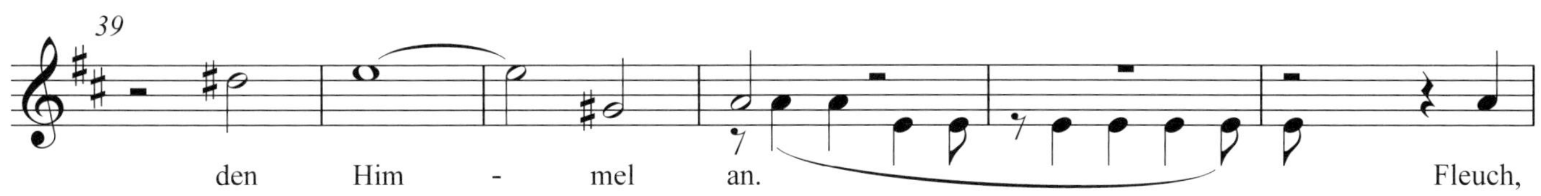
39
den   Him   -   mel   an.   Fleuch,

(a) notate melody
45
Nach - ti- gall, in grü-ne   Fin - ster nis - se, ins   Hain   - ge - sträuch,   und

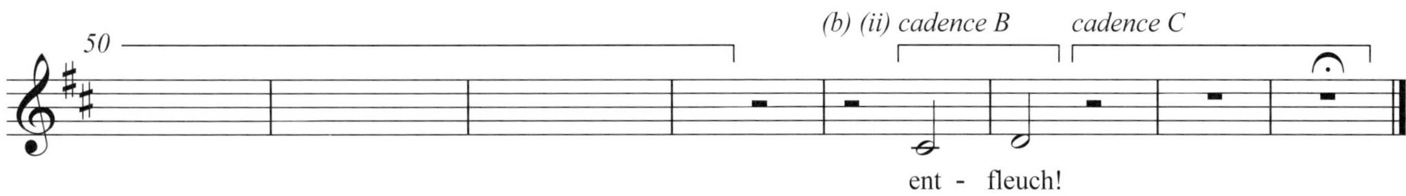
(b) (ii) cadence B   cadence C
50
ent - fleuch!

Test 4 (2011)

Allegro moderato
(b) (i)
cadence and key
f
p
(b) (ii) key
(b) (iii)
type of chord

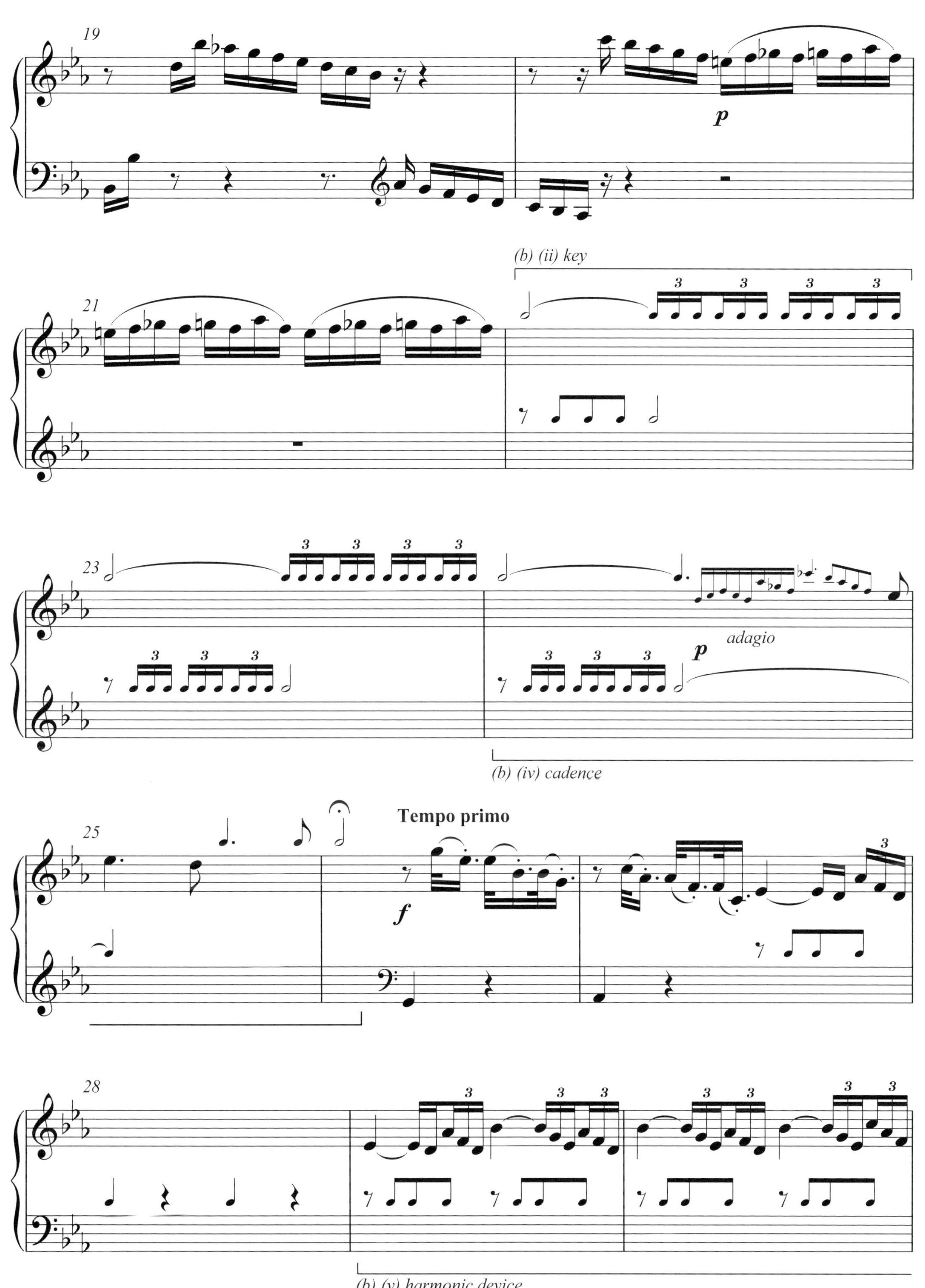
(b) (ii) key
(b) (iv) cadence
(b) (v) harmonic device
Tempo primo
adagio

(a) notate melody

Test 5 (2011)

Lento
1 (violin)
(b) (i) key and cadence
tr
3
5
6
(b) (ii) chord A
chord B
chord C
7
tr
(alto)
Er -
9
bar - me_ dich,____ er - bar - me dich, mein Gott, um mei - ner_ Zäh -
12
- - len wil - len, er - bar - me_ dich,____ er -
(a) notate melody
14
bar - - me, er - bar - me_ dich__ um
(b) (i) key and cadence
17
mei - ner - Zäh - ren, um mei - ner Zäh - ren_ wil - len,

Test 6 (2011)

Andante cantabile con moto
(a) notate melody
pp
(b) (i) chord A
chord B
sf
(b) (ii) key and cadence
p
(b) (iii) chord
p
tr
3

(b) (iv) key
f
sf   sf   sf
(b) (v) harmonic device

Track Order

A full track listing can be found on page 68.

Question 1: Comparison (2010)

Test 1. **A.** Vivaldi: Concerto in D minor, Op. 3 No. 11, movement II   0:00–0:57

      B. Vivaldi: Concerto in D minor, Op. 3 No. 11, movement III   0:00–0:52

Test 2. **A.** Beethoven: *Fidelio*, Act 1 No. 4 ('Hat man nicht auch Gold beineben')   0:00–1:01

      B. Beethoven: *Fidelio*, Act 1 No. 7 ('Ha! welch' ein Augenblick!')   0:00–1:03

Test 3. **A.** Stravinsky: Symphony in C, movement I   0:00–0:54

      B. Stravinsky: Symphony in C, movement IV   0:00–1:18

Test 4. **A.** Mendelssohn: Sonata in E, Op. 6, movement II   0:00–1:26

      B. Mendelssohn: Sonata in E, Op. 6, movement IV   0:00–1:25

Test 5. **A.** Morehouse and Trumbauer: *Three Blind Mice*   0:00–1:07

      B. Morehouse and Trumbauer: *Krazy Kat*   0:00–1:03

Question 1: Comparison (2011)

Test 1. **A.** Handel: *Let God Arise*, HWV 256b, movement III   0:00–1:11

      B. Handel: *Let God Arise*, HWV 256b, movement IV   0:00–1:06

Test 2. **A.** Bach: Brandenburg Concerto No. 1 in F, movement III   0:00–1:14

      B. Bach: Brandenburg Concerto No. 5 in D, movement III   0:00–1:16

Test 3. **A.** Schubert: Symphony No. 5, movement III   0:00–1:11

      B. Schubert: Symphony No. 9 (the 'Great C major'), movement III   0:00–1:07

Test 4. **A.** Bernstein: *West Side Story*, Act 1 No. 5 ('Maria')   0:00–1:33

      B. Bernstein: *West Side Story*, Act 2 No. 15 ('A Boy Like That')   0:00–1:12

Test 5. **A.** Debussy: 'Pagodes' from *Estampes*   0:00–1:21

      B. Debussy: 'Jimbo's Lullaby' from *Children's Corner*   0:00–1:22

Question 2: Aural Awareness (2010)

Test 1. Mozart: Agnus Dei from Mass in C, K. 317 — 0:00–2:39

Test 2. Haydn: Symphony No. 101 in D, movement I — 0:00–2:31

Test 3. Mozart: Piano Concerto No. 23 in A, K. 488, movement II — 0:00–2:17

Test 4. Weber: 'Kommt ein schlanker Bursch gegangen' from *Der Freischütz* — 0:00–2:19

Test 5. Mendelssohn: 'Venetianisches Gondellied' from *Lieder ohne Worte*, Op. 19 No. 6 — 0:00–2:42

Test 6. Vivaldi: 'Domine Deus, Agnus Dei' from *Gloria* — 0:00–2:27

Question 2: Aural Awareness (2011)

Test 1. Haydn: 'Now vanish before the holy beams' from *The Creation* — 0:00–1:44

Test 2. Bach: Fugue from Toccata and Fugue in F, BWV 540 — 0:00–2:23

Test 3. Brahms: 'An die Nachtigall' from *Vier Lieder*, Op. 46 — 0:00–2:47

Test 4. Haydn: Sonata in C minor, Hob. XVI: 20, movement I — 0:00–2:02

Test 5. Bach: 'Erbarme dich, mein Gott' from *St. Matthew Passion* — 0:00–2:19

Test 6. Beethoven: Symphony No. 1 in C major, movement II — 0:00–2:15

Answers

Question 1: Comparison (2010)

Test 1

Excerpt A: Vivaldi's Concerto in D minor, Op. 3 No. 11, movement II   0:00–0:57
Excerpt B: movement III   0:00–0:52

The work from which these excerpts are taken is one of twelve concertos published by Antonio Vivaldi (1678–1741) as *L'Estro Armonico* in Amsterdam in 1711, one of the most ambitious publishing ventures of the time, clearly aimed at spreading his music beyond Italy. Unlike many works in this collection, which were written for various solo combinations ranging from a single violin up to four violins and cello, the concerto in D minor chiefly employs the typical Corelli concertino of two violins and cello. Excerpt A is the opening of the second (slow) movement, which is in the manner of a siciliana. Excerpt B has the opening bars of the finale, with the vigorous string writing so characteristic of many quick movements by Vivaldi.

Related set works: Corelli's Trio Sonata in D, Op. 3 No. 2, movement IV (*NAM* 15) – Italian music of the mid to late Baroque; Tippett's Concerto for Double String Orchestra, movement I (*NAM* 6) – concerto.

(a)   Excerpt A: full strings <u>at first</u> (1), then <u>solo</u> violin (with legato melody) (1) plus <u>upper</u> strings (with detached chords) (1). Excerpt B: concertino/solo group (entering in imitation) <u>at first</u> (1) of two violins and cello (1) then with ripieno/accompanying group (1). Max. 3.

(b)   Concerto (grosso) (1). *Note*: both excerpts are from a concerto grosso, but the first includes a substantial passage for a solo violin, rather in the manner of a solo concerto, so that the answer 'concerto' without the adjective 'grosso' is acceptable. The dividing line between the different types of concerto was not always clear cut in Baroque times.

(c)   Excerpt A: melody-dominated homophony (1), accompanied by repeated chords (1). Excerpt B: imitative (at first) (1); (solo cello with) accompaniment of detached chords (1); solo violins in 3rds (1). Max. 2.

(d)   (i) TRUE (1); (ii) TRUE (1)

(e)   D (1)

(f)   Accept any year between 1690 and 1750 (1)

Test 2

Excerpt A: Beethoven's *Fidelio*, Act 1 No. 4 ('Hat man nicht auch Gold beineben')   0:00–1:01
Excerpt B: Act 1 No. 7 ('Ha! welch' ein Augenblick!')   0:00–1:03

Fidelio by Ludwig van Beethoven (1770–1827) belongs to a type of opera popular at the start of the 19th century in which the plot hinges on a rescue. Florestan is a political prisoner saved by his wife Leonora (who disguises herself as a boy, Fidelio). There is a scene of great poignancy at the beginning of Act 2, where Florestan, still in chains, sings of his pain, loneliness and imminent death. Florestan's desperate situation at that point might remind us to some small degree of Dido's in Act 3 of Purcell's *Dido and Aeneas*. Listen to Florestan's aria (from Act 2 of *Fidelio*) and Dido's lament (from Act 3 of *Dido and Aeneas*), and try comparing and contrasting the two composers' methods of depicting extremes of grief and desolation.

Related set works: 'Thy hand, Belinda' and 'When I am laid in earth' from Purcell's *Dido and Aeneas* (*NAM* 36) – opera; Beethoven's Septet in E♭, Op. 20, movement I (*NAM* 17) – music of Beethoven.

(a)   C (1)

(b)   Excerpt A is mostly limited in range/Excerpt B has wider range (1) and is (often) higher (1). Award (1) for any additional point about specific intervals, e.g. diminished 7th, octave and augmented 2nd. Phrasing in Excerpt A is periodic, phrasing in Excerpt B is irregular (1). Max. 2.

(c)   Excerpt A begins at a moderate(ly fast) speed (Allegro moderato) (1), slows to a pause (1), then becomes quicker (Allegro) (1), before ending with a final rall./rit. (1). Excerpt B is fast <u>throughout</u> (Allegro agitato) (1). Max. 2.

(d)   Diminished 7th chords (1); augmented 6th chords (1); dominant (minor) 9ths/diminished 7th chords <u>above</u> dominant in bass (1); augmented triad (heard once) (1). Max. 2.

(e)   Opera (1)

(f)   C (1)

(g)   A (1)

Test 3

Excerpt A: Stravinsky's Symphony in C, movement I   0:00–0:54
Excerpt B: movement IV   0:00–1:18

Igor Stravinsky (1882–1971) composed his Symphony in C in 1940 during the neoclassical phase of his career, which included *Pulcinella*, composed some 20 years previously. The symphony is not closely based on originals by other composers as *Pulcinella* was, but there is a debt to the past in the continued use of tonality (at a time when the way forward musically appeared to be increasingly atonal and serial), in a kind of emotional restraint which has clearer parallels in the Classical period than in Romantic music, and in apparent echoes of the celebrated four-note motif from Beethoven's Symphony No. 5.

Related set works: 'Sinfonia', 'Gavotta' and 'Vivo' from Stravinsky's *Pulcinella Suite* (*NAM* 7) *and* Tippett's Concerto for Double String Orchestra, movement I (*NAM* 6) – neoclassicism.

(a)   G (1)

(b)   Repeats whole figure (immediately, or from time to time within oboe melody)/alters intervals but not overall shape (e.g. to D, E, B)/sounds repeated Bs only (e.g. in timpani near beginning)/(rhythmic) augmentation (in bass or melody) (1).

(c)   (Mostly) stepwise (1) and within narrow (low) range (1); <u>opening</u> (three-note) <u>rising</u> pattern (1) inverted (1); a few leaps (1) including (perfect) 5ths (1). Max. 2. *Note*: reference to the two simultaneous melodic lines is more to do with texture than melodic writing, and need not be included here.

(d)   Oboe (1)

(e)   (Two) bassoon(s) (1) plus horns and/or trombones (1); (melody-dominated) homophony (1) with two simultaneous melodies (1) accompanied by detached chords (1). Max. 3.

(f)   Stravinsky (1). Accept instead any other composer of neoclassical orchestral music active in the middle years of the 20th century, e.g. Prokofiev, Tippett.

(g)   B (1)

Test 4

Excerpt A: Mendelssohn's Sonata in E, Op. 6, movement II   0:00–1:26
Excerpt B: movement IV   0:00–1:25

Felix Mendelssohn (1809–1847) composed his four-movement Sonata in E, Op. 6, in 1826 when (in 21st-century terms) he was in Year 12. The fourth movement in particular is very demanding technically – such virtuosity was widely expected and relished in the 19th century. However, the fast, lively music heard in Excerpt B is followed by a return to the tempo, mood and content of the first movement (an example of the cyclic treatment much loved by Romantic composers and already present in Beethoven's music).

Related set work: Nos. 1, 3 and 11 from Schumann's *Kinderscenen*, Op. 15 (*NAM* 23) – Romantic piano miniatures.

(a)   Excerpt A is in (simple) triple time (1); Excerpt B is in (simple) quadruple time (1). Excerpt A is built largely on a dotted-note pattern (1). Cross-rhythmic effects in A (1) – accept instead hemiola (1). Excerpt B has continuous shorter notes/semiquavers (1), and quaver-plus-two-semiquaver/long-plus-two-short patterns (1). Max. 4.

(b)   The opening passage (ending with two accented chords) is repeated (1). Repetition of two-/four-bar phrases (1) and use of sequence (1). Continuous (1) repetition of a short/rapid/three-note motif (with one longer note and two shorter ones) (1). Max. 2. *Note*: 'less repetitive' is too vague for a mark: try to make more positive remarks.

(c)   (i) Major (not minor as in Excerpt A) (1); (ii) Does not end in the tonic (as Excerpt A did)/ends (in supertonic minor) not in tonic (1).

(d)   B (1)

(e)   C (1)

Test 5

Excerpt A: *Three Blind Mice* by Morehouse and Trumbauer   0:00–1:07
Excerpt B: *Krazy Kat* by Morehouse and Trumbauer   0:00–1:03

Both excerpts feature the celebrated American jazz-cornet player Bix Beiderbecke (1903–1931), one of the first white jazz musicians to be highly regarded by black players. It was towards the end of the 20th century that Beiderbecke's full stature became apparent: this was aided by the appearance of the 1990 film *Bix: an interpretation of a legend*. Both excerpts are examples of Dixieland jazz, a type of traditional jazz that was based on the New Orleans style of the early 20th century.

Related set work: *West End Blues* by Louis Armstrong and his Hot Five (*NAM* 48) – early 20th-century jazz and blues.

(a)   Syncopation (1); swung rhythms (1)

(b)   Excerpt A (1)

(c)   Excerpt A: chordal/homophonic (1); reed(s)/sax(es) (1) in antiphony/call and response/alternation (1) with solo piano (1). Excerpt B: melody on cornet (1) accompanied by <u>detached</u> chords (1) on sax(es) (1). Max. 4.

(d)   Violin (1)

(e)   B (1)

(f)   B (1)

Question 1: Comparison (2011)

Test 1

Excerpt A: Handel's *Let God Arise*, HWV 256b, movement III 0:00–1:11
Excerpt B: movement IV 0:00–1:06

Anthems sung by present-day church choirs are usually fairly short pieces for choir and organ. Anthems by George Frideric Handel (1685–1759), composed after he had settled in England in the 1710s, are in several movements, include soloists as well as choir, and have orchestral accompaniment. Therefore in some ways they are similar to Bach's cantatas, but the texts are in English and chorales are not used. *Let God Arise* was originally written while Handel was composer to the Duke of Chandos, and is one of 12 'Chandos anthems'. The later version, on which this test is based, was revised for performance in King George I's Chapel Royal.

Related set work: Bach's Cantata No. 48, movements I–IV (*NAM* 28) – late Baroque choral music.

(a)   (Male) alto/countertenor (1) and bass/baritone (1) soloists (1). Max. 2.

(b)   Four-part (1) chorus/choir (1) including boys' voices/of boys' and men's voices (1). Max. 2.

(c)   Oboe (1)

(d)   Excerpt A: dialogue/imitation between solo parts (supported by continuo/bass)/duet plus accompaniment (1). Excerpt B: begins with octaves in choir (accompanied by bass) (1); where 'Hallelujah' begins texture is homophonic/chordal/antiphonal (1), followed by contrapuntal/imitative/fugal texture (1). Max. 2.

(e)   Anthem (1). Allow oratorio.

(f)   Handel (1). Allow Arne, Boyce or Purcell.

(g)   B (1)

Test 2

Excerpt A: Bach's Brandenburg Concerto No. 1 in F, movement III 0:00–1:14
Excerpt B: Bach's Brandenburg Concerto No. 5 in D, movement III 0:00–1:16

Brandenburg Concerto No. 5 by Johann Sebastian Bach (1685–1750) is a concerto grosso, the group of soloists comprising flute, violin and harpsichord. It was probably the first concerto ever to include a solo keyboard instrument; the harpsichord cadenza in the first movement is astonishing! Although sometimes classified as a concerto grosso, Brandenburg Concerto No. 1, with larger forces (including two horns and three oboes), is strictly an orchestral concerto. For more on the Brandenburg Concertos, see *Baroque Music in Focus* by Hugh Benham (Rhinegold, 2007).

Related set works: Bach's Cantata No. 48, movements I–IV (*NAM* 28) *and* Sarabande and Gigue from Bach's Partita No. 4 in D, BWV 828 (*NAM* 21) – music by Bach. Compare also the Fugue from Shostakovich's Prelude and Fugue in A, Op. 87 No. 7 (*NAM* 25) with the fugal third movement of Brandenburg Concerto No. 5.

(a)   (Two) horn(s) (1); (three) oboe(s) (1); bassoon (1); violin (1). Max. 2.

> The solo violin part is played on a violino piccolo, a small violin with a high range that was occasionally used by Bach and a few other composers of the Baroque period.

(b)   Excerpt A is melody-dominated homophony (1); Excerpt B is (mainly) fugal/imitative/contrapuntal (1). Additional detail may be rewarded, e.g. in Excerpt A, brief reductions to two parts (in middle and at end) (1); in Excerpt B many parallel 3rds (particularly in harpsichord) (1). Max. 2.

(c)   In Excerpt B it has a solo part (1); in Excerpt A it is part of the continuo/purely accompanimental (1).

(d)   Excerpt A opens with repeated notes (in oboes)/stepwise movement (in horns) (1); has an ascending shape in opening (i.e. fully-scored) phrase (1); followed by a <u>descending</u> sequence (in reduced texture) (1). Excerpt B opens with leap(s) of 4th (ascending and descending) (1); has an overall descending shape (in opening violin entry) (1); with an <u>ascending</u> sequence (based on three-note figure) (1). Max. 2.

(e)   Accept any year between 1700 and 1750 (1)

(f)   A (1)

Test 3

Excerpt A: Schubert's Symphony No. 5, movement III   0:00–1:11
Excerpt B: Schubert's Symphony No. 9 (the 'Great C major'), movement III   0:00–1:07

Symphony No. 5 by Franz Schubert (1797–1828) is an early work (1816), whereas the 'Great C major' was written towards the end of the composer's short life. No. 5, like some symphonies by Haydn and Mozart, uses a smallish orchestra without clarinets, timpani or brass other than horns. It still has a Minuet as the third movement (although, contrary to Classical practice, this is in the relative minor – an instance of Schubert's growing tonal freedom). The third movement of No. 9 is a Scherzo, a sign of Beethoven's influence, and indeed the work as a whole could not have been conceived without the example of that composer.

Related set works: Haydn's Symphony No. 26 in D minor, movement I (*NAM* 2) – symphony; Brahms' Piano Quintet in F minor, Op. 34, movement III (*NAM* 18) – scherzo.

(a)   In octaves (1); full orchestra/tutti/strings with woodwind and horns/brass (1)

(b)   (i) In octaves (also) (1); (ii) strings only (1)

(c)   Clarinet(s) (1)

(d)   Excerpt B starts/ends/is in a major key (1). Excerpt B ends in the dominant (not the tonic as in Excerpt A) (1); Excerpt A modulates to the relative major (1). Excerpt A visits only closely related keys (1), but Excerpt B passes through a more distant/(less closely related) (major) key (on the flattened leading note) (1). Excerpt B is more diatonic/lacks the (descending) (semitonal) chromatic movement in Excerpt A (1). Max. 2.

(e)   Scherzo (1)

(f)   Symphony (1)

(g)   C (1)

Test 4

Excerpt A: Act 1, No. 5 ('Maria') from Bernstein's *West Side Story*   0:00–1:33
Excerpt B: Act 2, No. 15 ('A Boy Like That')   0:00–1:12

Leonard Bernstein (1918–1990), a composer, conductor, pianist and teacher, was immensely versatile – equally at home in classical and popular styles. The plot of his celebrated musical *West Side Story* has much in common with Shakespeare's *Romeo and Juliet* (love transcends social rivalries, but with tragic results). In Excerpt A, Tony, a leading member of the Jets, is in love with Maria, sister of Bernardo, leader of the opposing gang, the Sharks. In Excerpt B, Anita (Bernardo's girlfriend) warns Maria against Tony. For more on *West Side Story*, see *Musicals in Focus* by Paul Terry (Rhinegold, second edition 2009).

Related set work: Bernstein's *On the Waterfront: Symphonic Suite* (opening) (*NAM* 43) – another example of the composer's versatility, this was originally music for film.

(a)   Excerpt A begins on a monotone/has repeated notes (1), Excerpt B has a wider range/includes lower notes (1). Excerpt A is diatonic, Excerpt B has some chromatic notes (1). Max. 2.

(b)   Excerpt A is in simple duple/quadruple time (throughout) (1), with (frequent) triplets (1). In Excerpt B the time signature alternates (1) between (simple) duple/quadruple and triple (1) (accept instead 'irregular metre'). Excerpt B has more frequent rests/shorter phrases/is more disjointed (1). (Prominent) habanera rhythm in (second half of) Excerpt A (1), with cross rhythms (between this and the triplets) (1). Syncopation in Excerpt B (1). Max. 3.

(c)   Excerpt A: major key/(upward) (tertiary) modulation or key shift/with raised fourth/Lydian inflections (1). Excerpt B: minor key/with some touches of major/tonal ambiguity (1).

(d)   Musical (1)

(e)   C (1)

(f)   A (1)

Test 5

Excerpt A: 'Pagodes' from Debussy's *Estampes*   0:00–1:21
Excerpt B: 'Jimbo's Lullaby' from Debussy's *Children's Corner*   0:00–1:22

'Pagodes' by Claude Debussy (1862–1918) is the first of the three *Estampes* ('Engravings') – a title that underlines the close relationship in Debussy's mind between the visual arts and music. Pagodas are those tall towers in Asia with several storeys, each storey having a projecting roof with upturned eaves. Debussy first became aware of music from Southeast Asia, including gamelan, at the 1889 Exposition Universelle (a kind of world fair) in Paris. *Children's Corner* is a suite of pieces written partly for the delight of Debussy's young daughter Claude-Emma. Jimbo (perhaps a misspelling of Jumbo) was her toy elephant: the low opening bars capture the animal's awkward movements perfectly.

Related set works: Sarabande and Gigue from Bach's Partita No. 4 in D, BWV 828 (*NAM* 21); Shostakovich's Prelude and Fugue in A, Op. 87 No. 7 (*NAM* 25) – examples of keyboard music, both earlier and later.

(a)   C (1). *Note*: in both excerpts the melody often employs only *four* notes from the pentatonic scale (the second, third, fourth and fifth – thereby avoiding the tonic), just as some gamelan melodies tend to favour four pitches from a five-note *slendro* scale.

(b)   Both use non-functional harmony (1), avoiding triads and their inversions (1). Chords are often built up from notes of the pentatonic scale (1), with major 2nds (1) prominent especially in Excerpt B (1). Harmonic rhythm/rate of chord change slow (1). Excerpt A has (double) pedal/tonic-and-dominant drone (at start) (1); Excerpt B has repeated, low tonic notes towards end (1). Max. 3.

(c)   Melody-dominated homophony (1), with melody at top (to start with) (1). <u>Later</u> melody (with longer notes) in middle of texture (1) in octaves (1), under (octave) triplets (1). Max. 2.

(d)   Monophonic/monophony (1)

(e)   Gamelan/Balinese/Javanese (1)

(f)   B (1)

(g)   Debussy (1). Accept instead Ravel.

Dictation Exercises

Test 1

11 note values to be supplied. Starting key: A major. If desired, the tonic chord (A–C♯–E) can be sounded before one or more playings of the test.

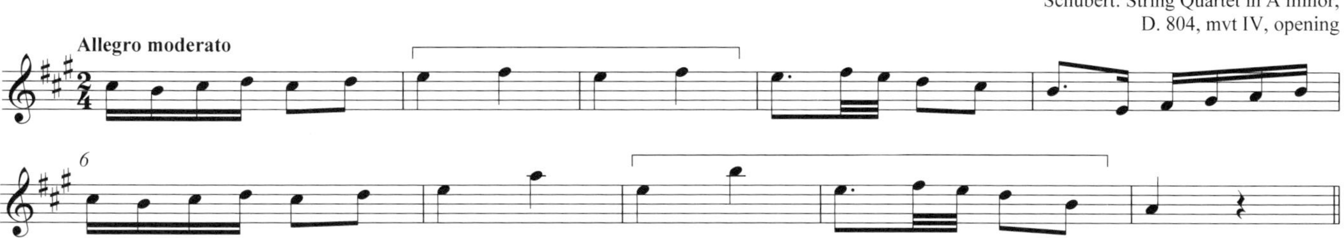

Test 2

10 pitches to be supplied. Starting key: B♭ major. See direction for test 1 on possible use of tonic chord.

Test 3

11 note values and 9 pitches to be supplied. Starting key: C major.

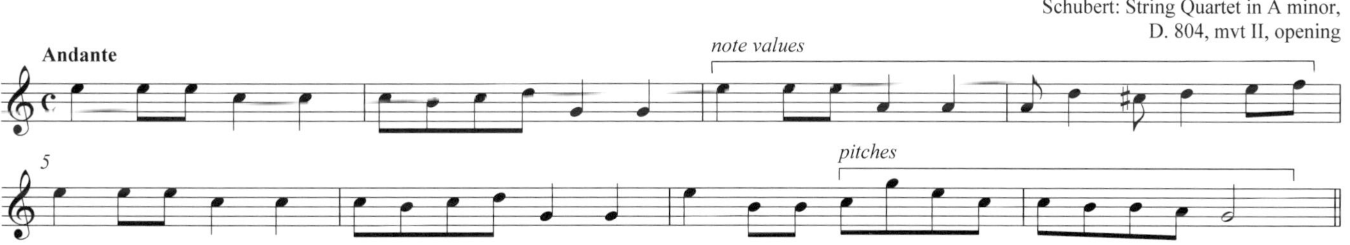

Test 4

8 note values and 9 pitches to be supplied. Starting key: C major.

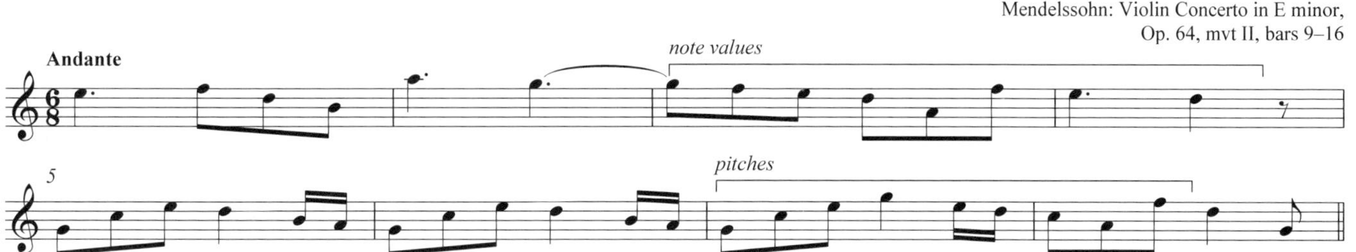

Test 5

8 note values and 13 pitches to be supplied. Starting key: F major.

Mozart: 'Ein Mädchen oder Weibchen' from
The Magic Flute (Act II, Scene V), bars 8–16

Test 6

10 notes to be supplied. Starting key: F major.

Telemann: Suite in F for 2 horns,
2 violins and bass, mvt II, opening

Test 7

10 notes to be supplied. Starting key: F major.

Telemann: Suite in F for 2 horns,
2 violins, and bass, mvt IV, bars 9–16

Test 8

9 notes to be supplied. Starting key: G minor.

Tchaikovsky: Violin Concerto in D,
Op. 35, mvt II, bars 17–20

Test 9

12 notes to be supplied. Starting key: G minor.

Grieg: 'Gjendine's Lullaby' from *19 Norwegian
Folk Tunes*, Op. 66, bars 9–13

Test 10

10 notes to be supplied. Starting key: B♭ major.

Test 11

10 notes to be supplied. Starting key: A minor.

Test 12

9 notes to be supplied. Starting key: B minor.

Test 13

9 notes to be supplied. Starting key: C minor.

Test 14

9 notes to be supplied. Starting key: D minor.

In bar 2 we hear ♩. ♪ followed by ♩ ⁊ ♪ – a subtle difference between the two. If possible, write the correct rests in dictation exercises, but sometimes it is difficult to be sure if a rest is there or not. In bar 2, if you wrote dotted crotchet and quaver twice over, this can be marked as correct.

Test 15

11 notes to be supplied. Starting key: E major.

Test 16

11 notes to be supplied. Starting key: A minor.

Test 17

8 notes to be supplied. Starting key: C minor.

Test 18

11 notes to be supplied. Starting key: E minor.

Test 19

11 notes to be supplied. Starting key: G minor.

Test 20

14 notes to be supplied. Starting key: D major.

This is quite difficult, partly because of the succession of short notes in bar 3 and the triplet in bar 4. It may be worth revisiting this and any other exercises you find difficult after some time.

Test 21

12 notes to be supplied. Starting key: E♭ major.

Question 2: Aural Awareness (2010)

Test 1

Excerpt: Agnus Dei from Mozart's Mass in C, K. 317   0:00–2:39

The music comes from the Mass in C (K. 317) by Wolfgang Amadeus Mozart (1756–1791), composed in Salzburg, Austria in 1779. This work, often referred to as the 'Coronation Mass', later accompanied imperial coronation ceremonies in the early 1790s. This test uses the beginning of the Agnus Dei, the final movement of the mass. The text means: 'Lamb of God, you who take away the sins of the world, have mercy on us'. Like most Roman Catholic church music composed in Austria in Mozart's time, the musical style is much influenced by secular (non-church) music.

Related set works: 'Thy hand, Belinda' and 'When I am laid in earth' from Purcell's *Dido and Aeneas* (*NAM* 36) – music for solo voice, and the operatic influence; Haydn's String Quartet in E♭, Op.33 No. 2, movement IV (*NAM* 16); Beethoven's Septet in E♭, Op. 20, movement I (*NAM* 17) – music in the Classical style.

(a)

There are 12 pitches and 12 note lengths to complete.

0	No work offered
1	1–3 pitches and/or note lengths correct
2	4–6 pitches and/or note lengths correct
3	7–9 pitches and/or note lengths correct
4	10–12 pitches and/or note lengths correct
5	13–15 pitches and note lengths correct
6	16–18 pitches and note lengths correct
7	19–21 pitches and note lengths correct
8	22–24 pitches and note lengths correct

(b)   (i)   Chord A: IIb/supertonic first inversion (1); chord B: Ic/tonic second inversion (1); chord C: V/dominant (1)

      (ii)   Bar 10: F (major)/tonic (1), perfect (1); bars 23–24: C major/dominant (1), perfect (1)

(c)   (i)   C (1)

      (ii)   Mozart (1). Accept instead Haydn.

      (iii)   B (1)

Test 2

Excerpt: Haydn's Symphony No. 101 in D, movement I   0:00–2:31

Symphony No. 101 in D major ('The Clock') was composed by Joseph Haydn (1732–1809) as one of a set of 'London' symphonies for his visit to England in 1794. The slow introduction, which is in the tonic minor key, helps to throw into relief the cheerful dance-like melody in 6/8 time that heads the main part of the movement. This is subtly linked to the Adagio by the rising scale with which each section begins. The nickname 'The Clock' was applied to the symphony because of the ticking effect of the pizzicato strings and staccato bassoons in the second movement.

Related set works: Haydn's String Quartet in E♭, Op.33 No. 2, movement IV (*NAM* 16) *and* Beethoven's Septet in E♭, Op. 20, movement I (*NAM* 17) – music in the Classical style.

(a)

There are 10 pitches and 10 note lengths to complete.

0	No work offered
1	1–2 pitches and/or note lengths correct
2	3–4 pitches and/or note lengths correct
3	5–7 pitches and/or note lengths correct
4	8–10 pitches and/or note lengths correct
5	11–13 pitches and note lengths correct
6	14–16 pitches and note lengths correct
7	17–18 pitches and note lengths correct
8	19–20 pitches and note lengths correct

(b) (i)   Chord A: Ic/tonic second inversion (1); chord B: V/dominant (1)

  (ii)   Bars 11–12: F major/relative major (1), perfect (1); bars 21–23: D minor/tonic (1), imperfect (1)

  (iii) Diminished seventh (1)

(c) (i)   Symphony (1)

  (ii)   D (1)

  (iii) Any year between 1770 and 1809 (1)

Test 3

Excerpt: Mozart's Piano Concerto No. 23 in A, K. 488, movement II   0:00–2:17

The music is from the second movement of Piano Concerto No. 23 in A (K. 488) by Wolfgang Amadeus Mozart (1756–1791), composed in 1786. Mozart was the earliest important composer of piano concertos, and to this day probably the most prolific. The solo parts, composed for himself to play, are not virtuosic in the manner of most 19th-century concertos, partly because late 18th-century instruments were far less strong in sound and construction than their successors. Accordingly the orchestra is also smaller, with the most powerful passages reserved for sections where there is no solo part. Mozart appears to have accompanied the orchestra in continuo fashion (especially where the piano part has only a single bass line), and he probably embellished or otherwise built on the notated solo part elsewhere. This test opens with a passage for piano solo, based on a lilting melody in $\frac{6}{8}$ time, almost in a pastoral style, but in an emotionally tense F♯ minor. The expected move to A major (the relative major) begins in bar 25; the shift to A *minor* shortly afterwards is both magical and slightly chilling.

Related set works: Tippett's Concerto for Double String Orchestra, movement I (*NAM* 6) – concerto; Haydn's String Quartet in E♭, Op.33 No. 2, movement IV (*NAM* 16) *and* Beethoven's Septet in E♭, Op. 20, movement I (*NAM* 17) – music in the Classical style.

(a) 

There are 11 pitches and 11 note lengths to complete.

0	No work offered
1	1–2 pitches and/or note lengths correct
2	3–5 pitches and/or note lengths correct
3	6–8 pitches and/or note lengths correct
4	9–11 pitches and/or note lengths correct
5	12–14 pitches and note lengths correct
6	15–17 pitches and note lengths correct
7	18–20 pitches and note lengths correct
8	21–22 pitches and note lengths correct

(b) (i)   Bar 6: appoggiatura (1); bar 14: suspension (1)

   (ii)   Chord A: Neapolitan sixth (1); chord B: Ic/tonic second inversion (1); chord C: V⁷/dominant seventh (1)

   (iii) A major/relative major (1)

   (iv)   Imperfect (1)

(c) (i)   (Piano) concerto (1)

   (ii)   D (1)

   (iii) B (1)

Test 4

Excerpt: 'Kommt ein schlanker Bursch gegangen' from Weber's *Der Freischütz*   0:00–2:19

This test is based on an excerpt from *Der Freischütz* (a title sometimes translated as 'The Marksman' or 'The Freeshooter') by Carl Maria von Weber (1786–1826). This work, commonly referred to as an opera, may also be called a *Singspiel*, a type of opera with German text and spoken dialogue between the musical numbers, of which Mozart's *Die Zauberflöte* ('The Magic Flute', 1791) is the best-known example. Our excerpt is the beginning of a song from Act II sung by the principal female character, Agathe. It is labelled 'arietta', meaning an operatic song that is shorter and/or lighter and less elaborate than a fully-fledged aria. *Der Freischütz* is an early example of Romanticism in music, as is demonstrated above all in the celebrated 'Wolf's Glen scene' (end of Act II) with its stunning depiction of the supernatural.

Related set work: 'Thy hand, Belinda' and 'When I am laid in earth' from Purcell's *Dido and Aeneas* (*NAM* 36) – opera.

(a)

There are 9 pitches and 9 note lengths to complete.

0	No work offered
1	1–2 pitches and/or note lengths correct
2	3–4 pitches and/or note lengths correct
3	5–6 pitches and/or note lengths correct
4	7–9 pitches and/or note lengths correct
5	10–12 pitches and note lengths correct
6	13–14 pitches and note lengths correct
7	15–16 pitches and note lengths correct
8	17–18 pitches and note lengths correct

(b) (i) Chord A: diminished seventh (1); chord B: dominant seventh (1)

(ii) F major/subdominant (1)

(iii) Bars 43–44: perfect (1), G major/dominant (1); bars 54–55: imperfect (1), A minor/relative minor (1)

(c) (i) Opera/Singspiel (1)

(ii) D (1)

(iii) D (1)

Test 5

Excerpt: 'Venetianisches Gondellied' from Mendelssohn's *Lieder ohne Worte*, Op. 19 No. 6   0:00–2:42

Test 5 is based on the 'Venetian Gondola Song' (Op. 19 No. 6) by Felix Mendelssohn (1809–1847). Composed in 1830, it is from the first of six sets of *Lieder ohne Worte* ('Songs without words'), in which the composer explored the lyrical potential of the piano without apparently ever having any words in mind. Mendelssohn entitled three pieces 'Venetian Gondola Song'; our example was actually composed in Venice. It was intended to recall the kind of songs (*barcarole*) that Venetian gondoliers sang at their work. Accordingly, like various 19th-century pieces called 'barcarolle', it is in $\frac{6}{8}$ time, with a lilting rhythm to suggest the movement of a boat through the water.

Related set work: Nos. 1, 3 and 11 from Schumann's *Kinderscenen*, Op. 15 (*NAM* 23) – Romantic piano miniatures.

(a)

There are 10 pitches and 10 note lengths to complete.

0	No work offered
1	1–2 pitches and/or note lengths correct
2	3–4 pitches and/or note lengths correct
3	5–7 pitches and/or note lengths correct
4	8–10 pitches and/or note lengths correct
5	11–13 pitches and note lengths correct
6	14–16 pitches and note lengths correct
7	17–18 pitches and note lengths correct
8	19–20 pitches and note lengths correct

(b) (i) Chord A: IVc/subdominant in second inversion (1); chord B: I/tonic (1)

(ii) C minor/subdominant (1)

(iii) Chord C: diminished seventh (1); chord D: (German) augmented sixth (1); chord E: V/dominant (1)

(iv) Appoggiatura (1)

(v) <u>Tonic</u> pedal (1)

(c) (i) C (1)

(ii) Any year between 1810 and 1850 (1)

Test 6

Excerpt: 'Domine Deus, Agnus Dei' from Vivaldi's *Gloria*   0:00–2:27

Test 6 is based on 'Domine Deus, Agnus Dei' ('Lord God, Lamb of God'), from the celebrated D major *Gloria* (RV 589) by Antonio Vivaldi (1678–1741). 'Gloria [in excelsis Deo]' ('Glory to God in the highest') is a Latin text from the principal Roman Catholic service, the Mass. While it was frequently set as the second movement of a multi-movement work (together with the Kyrie, Credo, Sanctus, Benedictus and Agnus Dei), Vivaldi's *Gloria* seems to have stood alone. However, it is not for his church music (nor indeed for his numerous operas) that Vivaldi is now best known. He wrote hundreds of concertos, including the so-called *Four Seasons*, helping to pioneer the three-movement (quick–slow–quick) design and ritornello form adopted by J. S. Bach, notably in the Brandenburg Concertos.

Related set works: 'Thy hand, Belinda' and 'When I am laid in earth' from Purcell's *Dido and Aeneas* (*NAM* 36) – Baroque writing for solo voice; Corelli's Trio Sonata in D, Op. 3 No. 2, movement IV (*NAM* 15) – Italian music of the mid to late Baroque.

(a)

There are 9 pitches and 9 note lengths to complete.

0	No work offered
1	1–2 pitches and/or note lengths correct
2	3–4 pitches and/or note lengths correct
3	5–6 pitches and/or note lengths correct
4	7–9 pitches and/or note lengths correct
5	10–12 pitches and note lengths correct
6	13–14 pitches and note lengths correct
7	15–16 pitches and note lengths correct
8	17–18 pitches and note lengths correct

(b)   (i)   Bars 8–9: D minor (1); bars 12–13: A minor (1). *Note*: in bar 8 (second minim beat) the diminished seventh (G♯–B♮–D–F) is chromatic: the G♯ and B♮ do not signify A minor.

(ii)   Bar 8: diminished seventh (1); bar 11: Neapolitan sixth (1)

(iii)   (Harmonic) sequence (a tone lower) (1). *Note*: Vivaldi manages to cadence in A♭ major at the end of the second passage – very far removed from the tonic key of D minor. The A♭ major chord in bar 19 does however in a sense point us ahead to the A♭ major chord at the end of bar 21, which is a Neapolitan sixth in G minor.

(iv)   Perfect (1)

(v)   Chord A: IVb/subdominant first inversion (1); chord B: V⁷/dominant seventh (1)

(c)   (i)   Mass (movement)/(a setting of) Gloria (in excelsis) (1)

(ii)   D (1)

Question 2: Aural Awareness (2011)

Test 1

Excerpt: 'Now vanish before the holy beams' from Haydn's *The Creation*   0:00–1:44

The music for this test is the beginning of the tenor aria 'Now vanish before the holy beams' from the oratorio *The Creation* (completed 1798) by Joseph Haydn (1732–1809). This work, originally with German text (as *Die Schöpfung*), quickly became popular in Britain. It tells of the creation of the universe, as described at the beginning of the first book of the Bible, Genesis, and in other texts from Milton's *Paradise Lost* and the Book of Psalms selected to comment on and amplify the Genesis account. Haydn's basic method is to use recitative for the biblical words, with arias and choruses for the additional text. The first non-biblical item is 'Now vanish'; the words, given to the archangel Uriel, refer to the banishing of primeval chaos by the creation of light, and the establishment of a wonderful and beautiful order. *The Creation* draws its inspiration partly from an 18th-century philosophical movement known as the Enlightenment, which emphasised reason, order and optimism.

Related set works: Bach's Cantata No. 48, movements I–IV (*NAM* 28) – sacred music; Haydn's Symphony No. 26 in D minor, movement I (*NAM* 2) – music by Haydn.

(a)

There are 12 pitches and 12 note lengths to complete.

0	No work offered
1	1–3 pitches and/or note lengths correct
2	4–6 pitches and/or note lengths correct
3	7–9 pitches and/or note lengths correct
4	10–12 pitches and/or note lengths correct
5	13–15 pitches and note lengths correct
6	16–18 pitches and note lengths correct
7	19–21 pitches and note lengths correct
8	22–24 pitches and note lengths correct

(b) (i) V^7 (1)

(ii)   Bars 11–12: A major (1), interrupted (1); bars 15–16: A major (1), perfect (1). *Note*: as so frequently in music of this style, a perfect cadence follows soon after an interrupted one, the function of the interrupted cadence being to prolong the phrase and keep us in suspense waiting for the almost inevitable perfect cadence. The interrupted cadence here has an interesting twist at the end: the chords are Ic–V^7–VI–*IVb*.

(iii)   Diminished seventh (1)

(iv)   (The second phrase) begins with I (not Ib)/the second chord (of the second phrase) is IV (not II^7b)/the third chord (of the second phrase) is V^7 (not V) (1)

(c) (i)   C (1)

(ii)   B (1)

(iii)   C (1)

Test 2

Excerpt: Fugue from Bach's Toccata and Fugue in F, BWV 540   0:00–2:23

Test 2 is the start of the Fugue from Toccata and Fugue in F, BWV 540 by J. S. Bach (1685–1750). Earlier organ toccatas, including those by Dieterich Buxtehude (1637–1707), tended to juxtapose fugal sections and showy semi-improvisatory passages. Bach's F major Toccata is non-fugal and less obviously showy, but very challenging with its pedal solos, constant semiquaver rhythm, and passages of intricate counterpoint. The Fugue begins with a slow-moving subject characterised by an initial chromatic descent. After our excerpt ends, a different, quicker subject is introduced; the piece ends with a masterly combination of the two subjects.

Related set works: Bach's Cantata No. 48, movements I–IV (*NAM* 28) – especially movement I with its contrapuntal artifice; Bach's Partita No. 4 in D, BWV 828 (*NAM* 21) – keyboard music by Bach; Shostakovich's Prelude and Fugue in A, Op. 87 No. 7 (*NAM* 25) – fugue; Brahms' Piano Quintet in F minor, Op. 34, movement III (*NAM* 18) – fugal writing.

(a) 

There are 10 pitches and 10 note lengths to complete.

0	No work offered
1	1–2 pitches and/or note lengths correct
2	3–4 pitches and/or note lengths correct
3	5–7 pitches and/or note lengths correct
4	8–10 pitches and/or note lengths correct
5	11–13 pitches and note lengths correct
6	14–16 pitches and note lengths correct
7	17–18 pitches and note lengths correct
8	19–20 pitches and note lengths correct

(b) (i)   Suspension (1)

    (ii)   Chord A: V⁷d/dominant seventh, third inversion (1); chord B: Ib/tonic first inversion (1)

    (iii) C major/dominant (1); perfect (1)

    (iv) Bars 46–48: B♭ major/subdominant (1); bar 62: G minor/supertonic minor/relative minor of subdominant (1)

    (v)   C major/dominant (1)

(c) (i)   Fugue (1)

    (ii)   A (1)

Test 3

Excerpt: 'An die Nachtigall' from Brahms' *Vier Lieder*, Op. 46   0:00–2:47

'An die Nachtigall', heard in full in this test, is the last of four songs by Johannes Brahms (1833–1897) published in 1868 as his *Vier Lieder*, Op. 46. The word 'lied' (singular of 'lieder') literally means just 'song', but is applied in particular to Romantic-period art songs with German text, for solo voice and piano (or less frequently orchestral) accompaniment. The expression 'art song' not only distinguishes a lied from operatic arias, folk and popular song, but also implies a particular subtle and sophisticated relationship between voice and accompaniment, and an intimate musical response to the mood and meaning of the text. Incidentally, the songs from Schoenberg's *Pierrot Lunaire* are not usually classified as lieder, but might be 'regarded as the tradition's culmination … exacerbating the expressive possibilities of both voice and accompaniment' ('Lied' in *Grove Music Online*).

Related set works: Bach's Cantata No. 48, movements I–IV (*NAM* 28) – settings of German text; 'Der kranke Mond' from Schoenberg's *Pierrot Lunaire* (*NAM* 40) – music for solo voice; Brahms' Piano Quintet in F minor, Op. 34, movement III (*NAM* 18) – music by Brahms.

(a)

There are 12 pitches and 12 note lengths to complete.

0	No work offered
1	1–3 pitches and/or note lengths correct
2	4–6 pitches and/or note lengths correct
3	7–9 pitches and/or note lengths correct
4	10–12 pitches and/or note lengths correct
5	13–15 pitches and note lengths correct
6	16–18 pitches and note lengths correct
7	19–21 pitches and note lengths correct
8	22–24 pitches and note lengths correct

(b) (i) II⁷b/supertonic seventh, first inversion (1)

   (ii) Cadence A: imperfect (1); cadence B: interrupted (1); cadence C: plagal (1). *Note*: plagal cadences are not widely used, but here we have one of the more common usages – after an interrupted cadence, to bring a piece or section to an end. Listen to the music again, and see if you can spot another interrupted cadence, this time fairly closely followed by an imperfect cadence (in D minor, in the phrase beginning 'von neuem' at bar 30).

   (iii) Bars 10–14: A major/dominant (1); bars 25–27: D major/tonic (1)

   (iv) <u>Dominant</u> pedal (1)

   (v) V (1)

(c) (i) C (1)

   (ii) Brahms (1). Accept instead another early/mid 19th-century composer of lieder, such as Schumann.

Test 4

Excerpt: Haydn's Sonata in C minor, Hob. XVI: 20, movement I   0:00–2:02

Joseph Haydn (1732–1809) composed numerous piano sonatas, the earlier ones as fairly straightforward teaching pieces. This test is based on the opening movement of Sonata No. 20 in C minor, which was apparently the first he called 'sonata' rather than 'divertimento' or 'partita'. It dates from 1771, and parts of it demonstrate an agitated style that can be found in other works, such as Haydn's Symphony No. 26 in D minor. This agitated style is often known as *Sturm und Drang* ('Storm and Stress'), although the term would not have been in Haydn's mind in 1771, for it originated as the title of a play written five years later by F. M. Klinger. When Haydn's sonata was published in 1780, one critic, while acknowledging its originality, complained of errors and harshness – a reminder that the views of critics on new music can, years afterwards, appear curiously misjudged to most people.

Related set works: Haydn's Symphony No. 26 in D minor, movement I (*NAM* 2) – music of the Classical period (specifically minor-key *Sturm und Drang* style); Bach's Partita No. 4 in D, BWV 828 (*NAM* 21); Shostakovich's Prelude and Fugue in A, Op. 87 No. 7 (*NAM* 25) – keyboard music.

(a) 

There are 10 pitches and 10 note lengths to complete.

0	No work offered
1	1–2 pitches and/or note lengths correct
2	3–4 pitches and/or note lengths correct
3	5–7 pitches and/or note lengths correct
4	8–10 pitches and/or note lengths correct
5	11–13 pitches and note lengths correct
6	14–16 pitches and note lengths correct
7	17–18 pitches and note lengths correct
8	19–20 pitches and note lengths correct

(b) (i) Perfect (1); C minor/tonic (1)

  (ii) Bars 12–14: B♭ major/relative major of dominant (1) (*Note*: varied sequence up a tone from A♭ major in bars 9–11); bar 22: E♭ major/relative major (1)

  (iii) Augmented sixth (1)

  (iv) Imperfect (1). *Note*: an unusual one – instead of ending on plain V, the last chord is a dominant 9th (B♭–A♭–D–C)!

  (v) <u>Dominant</u> pedal (1). *Note*: writing 'pedal' is not enough: precise identification means stating that the pedal is a dominant pedal.

(c) (i) Sonata (1)

  (ii) D (1)

  (iii) Accept any year from 1750 to 1800 (1)

Test 5

Excerpt: 'Erbarme dich, mein Gott' from Bach's *St. Matthew Passion*   0:00–2:19

The music for this test is from the alto aria 'Erbarme dich, mein Gott' ('Have pity, my God') from *St. Matthew Passion* by J. S. Bach (1685–1750). In the previous recitative Peter, Jesus' leading disciple, having just denied his master for the third time, is full of remorse and weeps bitterly. Bach then constructs a very extended aria of aching intensity on this single *Affekt*, never once cadencing in a major key. Among the expressive devices he uses are the Neapolitan sixth chord (first heard in bar 3) and some jagged melodic outlines, including augmented seconds (as in bar 5, A♯ to G♮). Bach's *St. Matthew Passion* is based on the Bible narrative of Jesus' suffering and death, but also includes non-Biblical words (such as 'Erbarme dich'). Although it is perfectly correct to call the work simply a 'Passion', the term 'oratorio Passion' is often preferred. See for example *Baroque Music in Focus* (Rhinegold, 2007), pages 66–68.

Related set works: Bach's Cantata No. 48, movements I–IV (*NAM* 28) – Bach's music for the Lutheran church; Bach's Partita No. 4 in D, BWV 828 (*NAM* 21).

(a)

There are 11 pitches and 11 note lengths to complete.

0	No work offered
1	1–2 pitches and/or note lengths correct
2	3–5 pitches and/or note lengths correct
3	6–8 pitches and/or note lengths correct
4	9–11 pitches and/or note lengths correct
5	12–14 pitches and note lengths correct
6	15–17 pitches and note lengths correct
7	18–20 pitches and note lengths correct
8	21–22 pitches and note lengths correct

(b)   (i)   Bar 4: B minor/tonic (1), imperfect (1); bar 18: F♯ minor/dominant (1), imperfect (1)

      (ii)   Chord A: IV/subdominant (1); chord B: Neapolitan sixth (1); chord C: V⁷d/dominant seventh, third invention (1)

(c)   (i)   D (1)

      (ii)   A (1)

      (iii) C (1)

Test 6

Excerpt: Beethoven's Symphony No. 1 in C major, movement II   0:00–2:15

The second movement of Symphony No. 1 in C major, Op. 21 by Ludwig van Beethoven (1770–1827) starts like a fugue, with a subject beginning C–F (dominant to tonic) played by second violins, and a tonal answer from violas and cellos on F–C (tonic to dominant). A further entry of the subject, in first violins doubled by woodwind at bar 12, forms part of a homophonic texture, with harmony entirely based on chords I and V⁷. So this is not to be a fugue after all, but a mostly light, dance-like movement (in sonata form). The two opening notes of the 'fugue' subject are however the source of much subtle humour later, not least as their interval is variously contracted (to a minor 3rd or even a minor 2nd) and expanded (up to a minor 7th), inverted and given different rhythmic emphases. Beethoven's ability to make a great deal out of tiny amounts of thematic material was one of the outstanding characteristics of his genius.

Related set works: Haydn's Symphony No. 26 in D minor, movement I (*NAM* 2) – symphony; Brahms' Piano Quintet in F minor, Op. 34, movement III (*NAM* 18) *and* Shostakovich's Prelude and Fugue in A, Op. 87 No. 7 (*NAM* 25) – fugal textures, for which see also Bach's Cantata No. 48, movements I–IV (*NAM* 28) – especially movement I, and Bach's Partita No. 4 in D, BWV 828 (*NAM* 21) – especially the Gigue.

(a)

There are 11 pitches and 11 note lengths to complete.

0	No work offered
1	1–2 pitches and/or note lengths correct
2	3–5 pitches and/or note lengths correct
3	6–8 pitches and/or note lengths correct
4	9–11 pitches and/or note lengths correct
5	12–14 pitches and note lengths correct
6	15–17 pitches and note lengths correct
7	18–20 pitches and note lengths correct
8	21–22 pitches and note lengths correct

If you add the melody line in bars 36–38, consult a score of the music for the answer.

(b) (i) Chord A: I/tonic (1); chord B: V⁷/dominant seventh (1)

    (ii) F major/tonic (1); imperfect (1). *Note*: this is not a plagal cadence in C, despite ending with chords of F and C major and having a B♮ (the briefest of auxiliary notes) in bar 24.

    (iii) Diminished seventh (1)

    (iv) A minor/mediant minor/relative minor of dominant (1)

    (v) <u>Dominant</u> pedal (1)

(c) (i) Imitation (1). Accept instead 'fugue' (as the writing has struck some writers as fugal in manner).

    (ii) Accept any year between 1780 and 1830 (1)

    (iii) B (1)

Section B: Music in Context

For Section B and C questions, it is impossible to give a totally comprehensive mark scheme that lists all the possible points students might make. Instead we have provided for each question what examiners call 'indicative content' – that is, a list of the main relevant points.

In every Section B answer you write, you should illustrate the points made with detailed references to the music under discussion, wherever appropriate. Such references will gain you additional credit. To see how this works, consult Edexcel's indicative content in the Sample Assessment Materials for Unit 6. For example, nine or more relevant, well-illustrated points will gain you the full 13 marks available for a Section B question, whereas nine or more relevant points with only limited illustration would be awarded nine or ten marks out of this 13-mark maximum.

> See also the *Edexcel A2 Music Revision Guide* (Rhinegold, 2010) for further examples of the holistic application of the mark scheme.

Applied Music 2010: Gabrieli

- ➢ 'Early' instruments required, e.g. cornett, early violin (close in range to modern viola), trombones
- ➢ Harmony involves:
  - ➢ Mainly root positions and first inversions
  - ➢ Cadences (Phrygian and plagal as well as perfect)
  - ➢ Suspensions, notably 4–3 and 7–6
  - ➢ Tierce de Picardie.

> These features are not exclusive to music such as Gabrieli's, but are typical of it and therefore it is appropriate to refer to them.

- ➢ Tonality is typical of Renaissance era:
  - ➢ Modal (Dorian on G)
  - ➢ Cadences on most degrees of the mode, resulting in considerable tonal variety.

Applied Music 2011: ET: Flying Theme

Rhythm
- ➢ Motor rhythms in introduction plus ostinato
- ➢ Repeated quavers in accompaniment to main theme.

Melody
- ➢ Sweeping theme with wide intervals (5th, 7th, octave) and common-chord framework
- ➢ Major mode, except for Lydian inflections (sharpened fourths) at bar 75 onwards.

Orchestration
- ➢ Exhilaration of experience emphasised by orchestration (bells, theme doubled across several octaves).

Section C: Continuity and Change in Instrumental Music

In every Section C answer you write, you should illustrate the points made with detailed references to the music under discussion, wherever appropriate. Such references will gain you additional credit. To see how this works, consult Edexcel's indicative content in the Sample Assessment Materials for Unit 6. For example, 18 or more relevant, well-illustrated points will secure you a mark in the outstanding category, i.e. 32–36 marks, whereas a similar number of relevant points without extensive illustration would gain you a mark of between 24 and 27 out of the 36-mark maximum.

Instrumental Music 2010

Melody
➤ **Beethoven:** periodic phrasing; frequent scalic lines; ornamentation; sequence
➤ **Armstrong:** improvisation; chromaticism; wide range overall; repetition
➤ **Tippett:** motivic; varying phrase lengths; various intervallic patterns, ranging from stepwise to more angular shapes; modality; inversion; sequence; ornamentation.

Harmony
➤ **Beethoven:** functional; perfect and imperfect cadences; varying harmonic rhythm; includes root, 1st and 2nd inversions, dominant 7ths and augmented 6ths
➤ **Armstrong:** twelve-bar blues harmonic progression; augmented triad at bar 6; substitution chords; decorated plagal cadence at close, consisting of $A\flat m^7 - E\flat^6$
➤ **Tippett:** rarely chordal textures; occasional cadences, including perfect and modal; final chord without a third; augmented triad, e.g. bar 124.

Instrumental Music 2011

Instrumentation
➤ **Haydn:** scored for small classical orchestra that still incorporates harpsichord
➤ **Brahms:** Romantic sound evident in use of piano and solo strings, all requiring considerable performance skill
➤ **Ellington:** typical of a transitional late-1920s style of jazz involving an ensemble larger than that found in earlier, more traditional jazz; some using 'jungle' style techniques.

Texture
➤ **Haydn:** chiefly homophonic (credit for details); first subject has a 'lean' two-part texture; pedals
➤ **Brahms:** wide range of textures including: octaves, imitation, fugato, melody-dominated homophony, homorhythm, pedals
➤ **Ellington:** mainly melody-dominated homophony with improvised melodies; stride textures in piano solo.

Full Track Listing

Question 1: Comparison (2010)

Test 1

Vivaldi: Concerto in D minor, Op. 3 No. 11, movement II   0:00–0:57
Vivaldi: Concerto in D minor, Op. 3 No. 11, movement III   0:00–0:52

The English Concert, Trevor Pinnock; *Vivaldi: L'estro armonico (Op. 3), 6 flute concertos (Op. 10)*
(DG Archiv 477 5421)

Test 2

Beethoven: *Fidelio*, Act 1 No. 4 ('Hat man nicht auch Gold beineben')   0:00–1:01
Beethoven: *Fidelio*, Act 1 No. 7 ('Ha! welch' ein Augenblick!')   0:00–1:03

London Symphony Orchestra, Colin Davis; *Beethoven: Fidelio* (LSO 0593)

Test 3

Stravinsky: Symphony in C, movement I   0:00–0:54
Stravinsky: Symphony in C, movement IV   0:00–1:18

Philharmonia Orchestra, Robert Craft; *Stravinsky: Symphony in C,
Symphony in Three Movements, Octet for Winds, Dumbarton Oaks Concerto* (Naxos 8.557507)

Test 4

Mendelssohn: Sonata in E, Op. 6, movement II   0:00–1:26
Mendelssohn: Sonata in E, Op. 6, movement IV   0:00–1:25

Frederic Chiu; *Mendelssohn: Piano Music* (Harmonia Mundi HCX3957117)

Test 5

Morehouse and Trumbauer: *Three Blind Mice*   0:00–1:07
Morehouse and Trumbauer: *Krazy Kat*   0:00–1:03

Bix Beiderbecke; *Jazz Masters: Bix Beiderbecke* (EMI CDMFP 6297)

Question 1: Comparison (2011)

Test 1

Handel: *Let God Arise*, HWV 256b, movement III	0:00–1:11
Handel: *Let God Arise*, HWV 256b, movement IV	0:00–1:06

Andrew Gant, Chapel Royal Choir; *Handel: Music for the Chapel Royal* (Naxos 8.557935)

Test 2

Bach: Brandenburg Concerto No. 1 in F, movement III	0:00–1:14
Bach: Brandenburg Concerto No. 5 in D, movement III	0:00–1:16

The English Concert, Trevor Pinnock; *Bach: Brandenburg Concertos Nos. 1–3* (DG Archiv 471720); *Bach: Brandenburgische Konzerte 4, 5, 6* (Archiv Produktion 410 501–2)

Test 3

Schubert: Symphony No. 5, movement III	0:00–1:11
Schubert: Symphony No. 9 (the 'Great C major'), movement III	0:00–1:07

New York Chamber Orchestra, Gerard Schwarz; *Schubert: Musically Speaking – Symphony No. 5, 'Unfinished' Symphony No. 8, German Dances* (Eroica Classical)

John Eliot Gardiner, Orchestre de l'Opéra de Lyon; *Schubert: Symphonies Nos. 8–9* (Erato)

Test 4

Bernstein: *West Side Story*, Act 1 No. 5 ('Maria')	0:00–1:33
Bernstein: *West Side Story*, Act 2 No. 15 ('A Boy Like That')	0:00–1:12

National Symphony Orchestra, Paul Manuel, Caroline O'Connor, Tinuke Olafimihan; *West Side Story (1993 Leicester Haymarket Theatre)* (TER 1197)

Test 5

Debussy: 'Pagodes' from *Estampes*	0:00–1:21
Debussy: 'Jimbo's Lullaby' from *Children's Corner*	0:00–1:22

Pascal Rogé; *Debussy: Children's Corner, Estampes, Suite Bergamasque* (ONYX 4018)

Question 2: Aural Awareness (2010)

Test 1

Mozart: Agnus Dei from Mass in C, K. 317 — 0:00–2:39

The English Concert and Choir, Trevor Pinnock; *Mozart: Coronation Mass* (DG Archiv 445 3532)

Test 2

Haydn: Symphony No. 101 in D, movement I — 0:00–2:31

Royal Philharmonic Orchestra, Jane Glover; *Haydn: Symphony No. 101 (The Clock), Symphony No. 103 (Drum Roll)* (Membran 222840)

Test 3

Mozart: Piano Concerto No. 23 in A, K. 488, movement II — 0:00–2:17

Alfred Brendel, The Academy of St. Martin in the Fields, Neville Marriner; *Mozart: Piano Concertos Nos. 21 and 23* (Decca)

Test 4

Weber: 'Kommt ein schlanker Bursch gegangen' from *Der Freischütz* — 0:00–2:19

Berliner Philharmoniker, Joseph Keilberth; *Weber: Der Freischütz* (EMI Classics 2088212)

Test 5

Mendelssohn: 'Venetianisches Gondellied' from *Lieder ohne Worte*, Op. 19 No. 6 — 0:00–2:42

András Schiff; *Mendelssohn: Piano Concertos Nos. 1–2, Songs without Words* (Decca 4664252)

Test 6

Vivaldi: 'Domine Deus, Agnus Dei' from *Gloria* — 0:00–2:27

Academy of St. Martin in the Fields, King's College Choir, Janet Baker, David Willcocks; *Haydn: Nelson Mass, Vivaldi: Gloria in D, Handel: Zadok the Priest* (Decca 4586232)

Question 2: Aural Awareness (2011)

Test 1

Haydn: 'Now vanish before the holy beams' from *The Creation* 0:00–1:44

Amor Artis Orchestra, Johannes Somary;
Haydn: Creation (Original 1797 English Text) (Newport Classics NPD 85627/2)

Test 2

Bach: Fugue from Toccata and Fugue in F, BWV 540 0:00–2:23

Walter Kraft; *Bach: Complete Organ Music* (Musical Concepts MC 191)

Test 3

Brahms: 'An die Nachtigall' from *Vier Lieder*, Op. 46 0:00–2:47

Bernarda Fink, Roger Vignoles; *Brahms: Lieder* (Harmonia Mundi HMC 901926)

Test 4

Haydn: Sonata in C minor, Hob. XVI: 20, movement I 0:00–2:02

Eva Mengelkoch; *Joseph Haydn: Piano Sonatas, Hob. XVI: 19, 20, 23, 32 and 50*
(Centaur Records CRC 2975/2976)

Test 5

Bach: 'Erbarme dich, mein Gott' from *St. Matthew Passion* 0:00–2:19

Geza Oberfrank, Hungarian Festival Choir, Hungarian State Symphony Orchestra,
Jozsef Mukk; *Bach: Favourite Arias and Choruses* (Naxos 8.553257)

Test 6

Beethoven: Symphony No. 1 in C major, movement II 0:00–2:15

Daniel Barenboim, Berliner Staatskapelle; *Beethoven: Symphonies Nos. 1–2* (Teldec 8573–83085–9)

Glossary

This glossary is not comprehensive: it refers to terms as used in this volume. For definitions of any common terms relating to tonality and harmony not included here (notably names of degrees of the scale such as dominant and leading note), see the AS Harmony Workbook *and/or the* A2 Harmony Workbook *(Rhinegold, 2008). More information on types of dissonance and types of chord are also available in these books. For fuller definitions of other terms and expressions, consult the* Dictionary of Music in Sound *(Rhinegold, 2002).*

Accidental. A symbol that changes the pitch of a note, usually by a semitone.

Affekt. German word meaning 'emotion' or 'mood'. Applied to a particular emotion or mood that lasts throughout a Baroque piece of music. Baroque composers (unlike those of the Classical period and later) often preferred to maintain a single *Affekt* throughout a movement rather than introduce marked changes of mood.

Anthem. A type of church music for choir, often accompanied by organ, and occasionally by larger forces. An anthem usually has English words (often from the Bible). In Church of England services, for which Handel wrote when he was in England, there are special places for anthems in the services of Morning and Evening Prayer (also known as Mattins and Evensong). *See also* **Verse anthem.**

Anticipation. A melody note (frequently the tonic of the key in the highest part) sounded slightly before the chord to which it belongs, thereby creating a dissonance with the previous chord.

Antiphony. Performance by different singers/instrumentalists in alternation. Often – but not always – the different groups perform similar material.

Appoggiatura. A non-chord note that sounds on the beat and then resolves by step (up or down a semitone or tone) to the main chord note. The dissonant note is not 'prepared' as a suspension is. Although appoggiaturas are normally approached by leap, accented passing notes that are particularly long and/ or prominent are often described as appoggiaturas, even though they are approached by step. Sometimes an appoggiatura, especially in music of the Classical period, is indicated by a note in small type, followed by its resolution printed at normal size.

Aria. A song, usually from an opera, oratorio or cantata, for solo voice, plus accompaniment for orchestra or, sometimes in Baroque times, for smaller forces, even just continuo. An aria often provides a character in an opera with the opportunity to reflect at length on their emotional state.

Atonal. Atonal music avoids keys or modes; that is, no pitch stands out consistently in the way that the tonic does in tonal music.

Augmentation. The lengthening of the rhythmic values of a previously-heard melody (e.g. where ♩ ♪ ♪ has become 𝅗𝅥 ♩ ♩).

Augmented interval. An interval that is one semitone wider than a major or perfect interval with the same number. For example, an augmented 5th (e.g. G–D♯) is one semitone wider than a perfect 5th (G–D); an augmented 4th (e.g. F–B) is one semitone wider than a perfect 4th (F–B♭).

Augmented-6th chord. A chromatic chord which in root position spans the interval of an augmented 6th, e.g. A♭–F♯. The chord also includes the major 3rd above the root (and sometimes also the perfect 5th or augmented 4th).

Auxiliary note. A non-chord note that occurs between, and is a tone or semitone above or below, two harmony notes of the same pitch.

Ballad. Originally a type of narrative verse, particularly from the British Isles, set in strophic fashion with the same music for each stanza. (Nowadays can just mean a love song.)

Baritone. A type of male voice higher than a bass and lower than a tenor.

Bebop. A style of jazz which developed in the 1940s from swing. More complex and less easy to dance to, it was characterised by improvisation, fast tempos, irregular phrase lengths and a greater emphasis on the rhythm section.

Cadence. A pair of chords signifying the end of a phrase in tonal music. Cadences are of several types, of which perfect and imperfect are by far the most common. *See also* **Imperfect cadence, Interrupted cadence, Perfect cadence, Phrygian cadence** and **Plagal cadence.**

Cadenza. A showy passage for a soloist, usually without accompaniment: sometimes long and most commonly found towards the end of the first movement of a concerto. Many 18th-century cadenzas sat between chords Ic and V in a perfect cadence (which is how the name 'cadenza' – Italian for 'cadence' – came to be applied). In the 18th century cadenzas were usually improvised, ending with a prolonged trill to provide a signal to the orchestra to re-enter.

Call and response. Originally signified a phrase sung by one person and answered by a different phrase sung by others. It is sometimes used as a synonym for antiphony. *See also* **Antiphony.**

Cantata. Usually a work for voice(s) and instruments in several movements. A cantata is generally shorter than an oratorio, sometimes without chorus, and can be sacred or secular. (In the early 17th century the term 'cantata' (Italian for 'sung') could be applied to more or less any sung piece.) *See also* **Oratorio**.

Chorale. A German hymn of the kind sung in the Lutheran (Protestant) church in the time of J. S. Bach. The word 'chorale' can refer to the words only, to the associated melody only, or to the whole hymn. Chorale melodies are largely stepwise (or conjunct); their harmonisation has long featured in advanced music courses.

Chordal. A form of homophony in which all the parts either move together in the same rhythm or have very limited independent rhythmic movement. The term **homorhythmic** (literally 'same rhythm') is sometimes used instead.

Chromatic. A chromatic note is one that does not belong to the scale of the key currently in use. For example, in D major the notes G♯ and C♮ are chromatic. The tonality of a passage containing many chromatic notes may be described as chromatic.

Compound time. A metre in which the main beat is subdivided into three equal portions. Opposite of **simple time**.

Concertino. The group of soloists in a Baroque concerto grosso – most commonly two violins and a cello (as in Corelli's Op. 6 concertos).

Concerto. Most commonly, a work for a soloist with orchestra. In many concertos the solo instrument is a piano or a violin. Occasionally there may be two soloists (a double concerto) or even three (a triple concerto). (In the 17th century the term was used more widely, and was applied originally to a work in which voices and instruments, with more or less independent parts, collaborated in a manner that was new at the time.) *See also* **Concerto grosso**.

Concerto grosso. A type of **concerto**, most common in the late Baroque period, in which three (or occasionally more) soloists, known as the **Concertino**, are contrasted with the sound of a larger group of mainly string instruments, known as the **Ripieno**.

Continuo. Short for 'basso continuo' (Italian for 'continuous bass'), and used chiefly in Baroque music. Refers to an instrumental bass line (most commonly played by cello(s), sometimes with bass(es)), together with an improvised accompaniment on keyboard or lute, which supplies full harmony that might otherwise be lacking.

Contrapuntal. Adjective to describe music that uses **counterpoint**. Counterpoint involves two or more melodic lines (usually rhythmically contrasted), each significant in itself, which are played or sung together – in contrast to **homophony**, in which one part has the melody and the other parts accompany. The term 'polyphonic' is often used as a synonym for contrapuntal.

Counterpoint. *See* **Contrapuntal**.

Countertenor. A type of adult male voice higher than a tenor, which often involves use of a special high vocal register known as falsetto. The term 'male alto' is sometimes employed for those countertenors who use the falsetto register.

Cross-rhythm. The use of two or more very different rhythms simultaneously in different parts. One rhythm may imply one metre (or time signature), while another implies a different one.

Cyclic. Cyclic treatment involves the use of the same thematic material in two or more movements (usually of a sonata or symphony).

Diatonic. Using notes that belong to the current key. A diatonic note is one that belongs to the scale of the key currently in use. For example, in D major the notes D, E and F♯ are diatonic.

Diminished-7th chord. A dissonant four-note chord made up of super-imposed minor 3rds (for example C♯–E–G–B♭).

Dissonance. Any note not a major or minor 3rd or 6th, perfect 5th, unison or perfect octave above the lowest part sounding is strictly a dissonance. Triads in root position or in first inversion are therefore the only chords that have no dissonance. (Even the fourth above the bass in a second inversion counts as dissonant.) Some dissonances, particularly suspensions and appoggiaturas, add harmonic tension and can help make the music more expressive; others, notably passing and auxiliary notes, provide rhythmic and melodic decoration. Although 'dissonance' and 'discord' are in some ways similar, dissonance is usually more to do with tension than with any deliberate roughness or harshness of sound that might be implied by the word discord.

Dixieland. A name given to traditional jazz, particularly when played by white musicians in the period between about 1917 and 1930, although also used for later revivals of the style. It lacked some of the feeling for swung rhythms and blues inflections characteristic of early black jazz, but helped to extend the melodic and harmonic vocabulary of jazz.

Dominant 7th. A dissonant four-note chord built on the dominant note of the scale. It includes the dominant triad plus a minor 7th above the root.

Dorian mode. A scale that uses the following pattern of tones (T) and semitones (s): T–s–T–T–T–s–T. When starting on D, it consists of all the white notes within one octave on a keyboard.

First inversion. *See* **Inversion**.

Fugal. *See* **Fugue.**

Fugato. A passage in fugal style which forms part of a larger piece of music.

Fugue. A type of piece in which a theme called a 'subject' is treated in imitation by all the parts (usually with short passages called 'episodes' from which it is absent, for relief and contrast). The adjective is **fugal** (for instance, 'in fugal style' means 'in the style of a fugue').

Functional harmony. A type of harmony that has the *function* of defining a major or minor key, in particular through chords on the tonic and dominant (I and $V^{(7)}$), with special emphasis on perfect cadences ($V^{(7)}$–I).

Gamelan. An ensemble from Indonesia (usually from Bali or Java) consisting largely of tuned percussion.

Genre. A type of music. Genres include the sonata, the string quartet and the symphony.

Harmonic rhythm. The rate at which harmony changes in a piece.

Hemiola. The articulation of two units of triple time (strong–weak–weak, strong–weak–weak) as three units of duple time (strong–weak, strong–weak, strong–weak).

Homophony. A texture in which one part has a melody and the other parts accompany, in contrast to contrapuntal writing, where each part has independent melodic and rhythmic interest.

Homorhythm. *See* **Chordal.**

Imitation. Where a melodic idea in one part is immediately repeated in another part (exactly or inexactly), at the same or a different pitch, while the first part continues. The adjective is 'imitative'.

Imperfect cadence. An open-ended or inconclusive cadence ending with the dominant chord (V). The preceding chord is usually I, ii or IV.

Improvisation. The process of spontaneously creating new music, often basing this on existing musical material (such as a chord pattern) – in effect, it means performing music as you compose it. Improvisation is very common in jazz.

Instrumentation. The choice of instruments for a piece of music. (The expression 'instrumental forces' is sometimes used instead.)

Interrupted cadence. A cadence intended to create surprise or suspense, perhaps by delaying the arrival of a final perfect or plagal cadence. Usually an interrupted cadence consists of chord V followed by chord VI.

Inversion. When a chord has a note other than the root in the lowest part, it is an inversion. In a first-inversion chord the 3rd of the chord is in the lowest part, and in a second-inversion chord the 5th. For example, a triad of F major in first inversion is A–C–F, and in second inversion is C–F–A. *See also* **Root position.**

Jungle. A style of jazz developed by Duke Ellington in the 1920s, characterised especially by dark textures and growling brass effects.

Lied (plural lieder). German for song, but used in English to refer specifically to 19th-century settings of German poetry for an accompanied solo voice.

Lydian mode/inflections. The Lydian mode is a scale that uses the following pattern of tones (T) and semitones (s): T–T–T–s–T–T–s. When starting on F, it consists of all the white notes within one octave on a keyboard. We speak of Lydian 'inflections' when music in F major has occasional B♮(s) in a manner characteristic of the Lydian mode.

Magnificat. The words of the Virgin Mary before the birth of Jesus (from the gospel of Luke, chapter 1), widely sung in church services, including the Church of England service of Evening Prayer or Evensong. 'Magnificat' is the first word of the Latin version of this song.

Mass. The Mass is the principal service of the Roman Catholic church; it corresponds in some ways with services of Holy Communion in other churches. The word 'mass' (often, as here, with a lower-case 'm') can also refer to a musical setting of certain texts from the Mass (for example, Gloria in excelsis and Sanctus).

Melody-dominated homophony. As with 'ordinary' homophony, a texture in which one part has a melody and the other parts accompany. With melody-dominated homophony, however, the melody stands apart from the accompaniment particularly clearly and strongly.

Metre. Concerns the identity, grouping and subdivision of beats, as indicated by a time signature. E.g. the time signature $\frac{3}{4}$ indicates a simple triple metre, in which each bar consists of three crotchet beats, any of which can be divided into two quavers. In contrast, $\frac{9}{8}$ is a compound triple metre, in which each bar consists of three dotted-crotchet beats, any of which can be divided into three quavers.

Minuet. A dance in simple triple metre of French origin. 17th- and 18th-century composers often included pieces entitled minuet in suites and symphonies, but for listening to, not for dancing. A minuet was generally played through twice, with, in between, a 'trio' (another minuet in all but name). Most minuets were graceful and not very fast. *See also* **Scherzo.**

Modal. A term often used to refer to music based on a mode rather than on major and minor keys.

Modulation. A change of key, or the process of changing key.

Monophony. Music consisting only of a single melodic line. The adjective is 'monophonic'.

Motet. A type of church music for choir, sometimes accompanied by organ, and occasionally by larger forces. A motet often has Latin words (commonly from the Bible), and is particularly but not exclusively associated with Roman Catholic services.

Motif. A short but distinctive musical idea that is developed in various ways in order to create a longer passage of music. The adjective is '**motivic**' (e.g. 'motivic development' means 'development of a motif'.)

Motivic. *See* **Motif**.

Neapolitan-sixth chord. A chromatic chord (often in a minor key) consisting of the first inversion of the major chord formed on the flattened supertonic, i.e. the flattened second degree of the scale (in D minor, for example, the Neapolitan sixth has the notes G–B♭–E♭).

Neoclassical. A term used for music in which the composer revives elements from an earlier style (not necessarily a Classical one). These elements normally exist alongside more up-to-date ones – mere copying of an old style is 'pastiche'.

Opera. A large-scale dramatic work for singers and instrumentalists. In most cases the whole text is sung, so that an opera is very different from a play with incidental music. An opera differs from a musical too (for example, the music is not generally popular in idiom).

Oratorio. A large-scale work on a religious subject for solo voice(s), chorus and instruments in a number of movements. *See also* **Cantata**.

Ornamentation. Addition of melodic decoration, often through the use of conventional forms of ornamentation such as trills and mordents.

Ostinato. A repeating melodic, harmonic or rhythmic motif, heard continuously throughout part or the whole of a piece.

Parallel 3rds. Parallel 3rds occur where two parts that are a 3rd apart move together in the same direction to another 3rd. Such movement can be up or down; it is commonly, but not necessarily, by step.

Passing note. A non-harmony note approached and quitted by step in the same direction, often filling in a melodic gap of a 3rd (e.g. A between G and B, where both G and B are harmony notes).

Passion. A musical setting of the story of the sufferings and death on the cross of Jesus Christ as told in the New Testament of the Bible. An oratorio Passion is one which, like Bach's St

Matthew, includes non-biblical words in addition to those of the biblical narrative.

Pedal (note). A sustained or repeated note, usually in a low register, over which changing harmonies occur. A pedal on the fifth note of the scale (a dominant pedal) tends to create a sense of expectation in advance of a perfect cadence; a pedal on the keynote (a tonic pedal) can create a feeling of repose.

Perfect cadence. A cadence ending with the tonic chord (I), preceded by the dominant (V or V⁷) – appropriate where some degree of finality is required.

Periodic phrasing. Phrases of regular length (two- and four-bar phrases, and multiples thereof) are deliberately combined to form balanced larger units, sometimes with a clear sense of 'question and answer' or 'antecedent and consequent'. Particularly found in Classical-period music.

Pentatonic. A scale made up of five notes, most frequently the first, second, third, fifth and sixth degrees of a major scale (for example, the major pentatonic scale of C is C–D–E–G–A).

Phrygian cadence. A type of imperfect cadence, in which the dominant chord (V) is preceded by the first inversion of the subdominant (IVb). It is used chiefly in minor keys, and particularly in Baroque music.

Pivot chord. A chord that links together two different keys in a modulation and is common to both of them. For example, the chord of D minor is found in the keys of F and C, and so can be used as a pivot chord in a modulation from F to the dominant.

Pizzicato (abbreviated to pizz.). A direction to pluck, instead of bow, string(s) on a violin, viola, cello or double bass. Cancelled by the direction 'arco' – with the bow.

Plagal cadence. A cadence ending with the tonic chord (I), preceded by the subdominant (IV). Appropriate where a restful finality is required, it is used sparingly in tonal music.

Ragtime. A style of popular music that emerged in the 1890s and continued throughout the first two decades of the 20th century. It is usually in $\frac{2}{4}$ time and is characterised by a syncopated melody played against a march-like accompaniment.

Range. The interval between the lowest note in a passage and the highest (for example, a melody with middle C as lowest note and C in the third space of the treble stave as highest note has a range of an octave).

Relative major and minor. Keys that have the same key signature but a different scale (e.g. F major and D minor, both with a key signature of one flat). A relative minor is three semitones lower than its relative major (e.g. the tonic of D minor is three semitones lower than the tonic of its relative major, F major).

Ripieno. The players other than the soloists in a Baroque concerto grosso. (Italian for 'filling up' or 'completion'.)

Ritornello form. A structure used in Baroque music in which an opening instrumental section (called the ritornello) introduces the main musical ideas. This returns, often in shortened versions and in related keys, between passages for one or more soloists. The complete ritornello (or a substantial part of it) returns in the tonic key at the end.

Root position. A chord which has the root in the lowest sounding part.

Scherzo. A fast movement which, from the early 19th century, usually replaced the minuet in a symphony or sonata. It is generally similar in structure to a minuet (with a contrasting trio), and usually in simple triple time; but there are several examples in duple time by later Romantic composers, for example the Brahms scherzo in *NAM* (no. 18, page 231) which alternates between compound duple ($\frac{6}{8}$) and simple duple ($\frac{2}{4}$).

Second inversion. *See* **Inversion**.

Sequence. Immediate repetition of a melodic or harmonic idea at a different pitch.

Serial. In serial music all (or most) pitches are derived from an underlying fixed series of pitches which can be manipulated by transposition, inversion and retrograding (being played backwards). A widely practised form of serialism in the mid 20th century used a series (or 'row') of twelve notes that included every note of the chromatic scale once.

Siciliana. A type of instrumental or vocal movement popular in the 17th and 18th centuries, often used to suggest pastoral scenes. Normally fairly slow and in compound time ($\frac{6}{8}$ or $\frac{12}{8}$).

Simple time. A metre in which the main beat is sub-divided into two equal portions. Opposite of **compound time**.

Singspiel. An opera with German words, some of which are spoken not sung. Most singspiels are from the late 18th and early 19th centuries, and the comic element is often strong. ('Singspiel' is German for 'sung play'.) *See also* **Opera**.

Sonata. An instrumental work, commonly in three or four movements. From the late Baroque period onwards, sonatas are usually for solo keyboard or for single melody instrument and keyboard. 'Trio sonatas' (middle to late Baroque) are normally for two violins and continuo. In the early Baroque, 'sonata' meant little more than a piece that was played (literally 'sounded') not sung.

Sonata form. A form developed in the Classical period from binary form. The first section is the exposition, beginning in the tonic and ending in a closely-related key, often with two contrasting groups of melodic material (first subject, second subject). The second section commonly includes a development section, followed by a recapitulation with first and second subjects restated in the tonic. Sonata form is used generally for the first quick movement from a Classical or post-Classical symphony or sonata, and sometimes also for other movements.

Stride. A jazz piano style partly derived from ragtime, in particular from the characteristic left-hand pattern which repeatedly 'strides' from a low note or chord on a strong beat to a higher chord on a weak beat. Stride piano was particularly popular in the 1920s.

Substitution chord. A chord, especially in jazz, used to replace one of the chords in a harmonic progression. It has a similar harmonic function to the chord it replaces, and may have one or more notes in common with it. For example, in Ellington's *Black and Tan Fantasy* (*NAM* 49), the B♭ major 12-bar blues (bars 29–40) has a Cm⁷ chord (C–E♭–G–B♭) in bar 37 in place of the expected E♭ chord (E♭–G–B♭).

Suspension. A suspension occurs at a change of chord, when one part hangs on to (or repeats) a note from the old chord, creating a dissonance, after which the delayed part resolves by step (usually down) to a note of the new chord.

Swung rhythm. In jazz and other popular music, a certain freedom in performance whereby rhythms that might in other contexts be played 'straight' (as equal notes) are performed with the first of each pair longer than the second, often with a kind of triplet effect.

Syncopation. The shifting of stress from a strong to a weak beat. For example, in a $\frac{4}{4}$ bar with the rhythm ♩ ♩ ♩, the minim (a relatively long note beginning on a weak beat) is syncopated.

Symphony. A work for orchestra with several (usually three or four) movements in different tempi – in effect a sonata for orchestra rather than for one or a few instruments.

Texture. The relationship between the various simultaneous lines in a passage of music, dependent on such features as the number and function of the parts and the spacing between them.

Tierce de Picardie. A major 3rd in the final tonic chord of a passage in a minor key.

Tonality. The system of major and minor keys in which one note (the tonic, or key note) has particular importance, and in which various keys are related. Especially in the 18th and 19th centuries, tonality is established by the use of **functional harmony**. For exam purposes, questions on tonality might also include identifying music that is modal (based on one or more modes) or that is based on non-western scales. Western music that uses neither keys nor modes is described as atonal (without tonality).

Tutti. Used in orchestral scores to show that everyone is required to play, not just soloist(s) or other reduced forces.

(Italian for 'all'.)

Triplet. A group of three equal notes played in the time normally taken by two notes of the same type. For example, a triplet of quavers is played in the time taken by two normal quavers.

Twelve-bar blues. A standard chord sequence lasting 12 bars, used in the blues and other popular music. It is based on the tonic (I), subdominant (IV) and dominant (V) chords of a key. A common form is I–I–I–I, IV–IV–I–I, V–IV–I–I.

Unison. Simultaneous performance of the same note or melody by two or more players or singers.

Verse anthem. *See* **Anthem**. In a verse anthem sections for soloist(s) alternate with those for the full choir.

Violino piccolo. In Baroque times, a type of small violin tuned higher than an ordinary violin (by a 3rd or a 4th), thus making it easier to play high notes. (Italian for 'small violin'.)

Whole-tone scale. A scale in which the interval between every successive note is a whole tone.